Ghosts Among Us

Also by Leslie Rule

Coast to Coast Ghosts: True Stories of Hauntings Across America

Ghosts Among Us

True Stories of Spirit Encounters

Leslie Rule

Andrews McMeel
Publishing

Kansas City

07 08 RR4 10 9 8

Library of Congress Cataloging-in-Publication Data
Rule, Leslie, 1958–
    Ghosts among us : true stories of spirit encounters /
Leslie Rule.
        p. cm.
    ISBN-13: 978-0-7407-4717-5
    ISBN-10: 0-7407-4717-7
        1. Ghosts. I. Title.

BF1461.R78 2004
133.1—dc22
                                        2004048058

Book design by Holly Camerlinck

Attention Schools and Businesses:
Andrews McMeel books are available at quantity discounts
with bulk purchase for educational, business, or sales
promotional use. For information, please write to: Special
Sales Department, Andrews McMeel Publishing, LLC, 4520
Main Street, Kansas City, Missouri 64111.

This book is for Teresa Grandon-Garcia,
my friend for over three decades.
She has shown amazing strength and optimism
in her recent struggle with cancer.
Teresa, may you grow stronger every day!

Contents

Foreword by Ann Rule

I suspect that, if they would admit it, most people have a certain fascination with ghosts, spirits, angels, guides—whatever words they may use to describe otherworldly presences in their lives. Sometimes, it is a feeling of an unseen presence, a sound in the room with no rational explanation, a phone ringing when it is not connected to the wall, or even a thought washing through the brain, unbidden.

For over thirty years, I have researched and written about the lives of people I didn't know—that I could never know. The subjects of the twenty-three books and over a thousand articles I have written are dead, and almost all of them died violently. I write about murder cases. If anything could make me believe in ghosts, it is the genre in which I write. It may sound bizarre, but I grow to know my subjects better than anyone who knew them in life. I have heard homicide investigators say the same thing.

As I work now on *Green River, Running Red,* the true story of a stalking killer who has admitted to taking forty-eight young women's lives, the dead girls seem to come and go in my office. I have learned their secrets, their fears, their hopes, all the things that ended prematurely at the whim of a person without conscience. I know their blood types and their DNA patterns. I've seen broken pieces of their pathetically inexpensive jewelry, caked with mud. I have, quite literally, knelt next to their unmarked graves.

Their presence doesn't bother me. Instead, it helps me to put my hand on exactly the report I'm looking for at a given time. Bear in mind that I have more than fifty thousand pages of interviews, evidence, and police follow-up pages. If I didn't have some "help" from the victims, I think I might be paralyzed with indecision as I try to access the information I need.

Although I always try to tell the whole story of a murder case—from the police probe to the trial, and, sometimes, to the final moment of a death penalty, the most important thing I do is try to speak for the victims. A high-profile murder suspect is assured of becoming a pseudo-celebrity. He will have his chance to be on television screens across America and in the headlines of newspapers and tabloids. He can tell his story from the witness stand in a court of law. If he's really infamous, he will surely have producers anxious to film a miniseries or two about his life.

The victims don't have that. Because they are dead and gone, they appear in one-dimensional photographs, and they cannot tell what really happened during the last moments of their lives. Someone else must speak for them, whether it's a district attorney or a witness for the prosecution. Or someone like me.

It is not at all unusual for homicide victims to come back with messages for the people they never got to say good-bye to. So many of their parents have told me of dreams that were much too real to be just dreams. Only yesterday, a mother spoke to me about how her daughter came to her at a time when her grief was so intense that she thought she herself would die of the pain.

"It was in a dream—a wonderful dream. She smiled her wonderful smile and touched my arm. She told me that everything was all right. That she was fine and that I must not cry. It was going to be okay, even though I might not believe her right away."

When the mourning mother woke up, she didn't know if her waking state was reality, or if the lovely dream was the real world. She would certainly have grief and pain for the rest of her life because her daughter was gone, but she was also left with the absolute belief that one day her lost child would come back for her and help her to cross over.

Because I spend my days thinking about how thin the dividers are between life and death—and not in a morbid way, at all—I am probably more receptive to ghostly visitors than most people are. And I think it makes it easier for people to tell me their own ghost stories. They know I won't laugh at them or think they don't have "both oars in the water."

It's been thirty years since a pretty blue-eyed thirteen-year-old girl named Janna left her mother's apartment to walk down a path to the grounds of a lodge and a golf course where her best friend lived in a mobile home. Janna had promised to water the plants and check to be sure the pipes wouldn't freeze while her friend and her family were away on a Christmas visit.

Detectives were able to determine that Janna did arrive at the trailer, but she never came home. She completely disappeared that morning. Although the investigators followed every lead they could glean, they couldn't find Janna. Some people said she'd run away, but her mother knew she had no reason to do that. Theirs was a happy home and she and Janna had been planning to have lunch together on the day her daughter vanished. No arguments. No fights. No problems.

Desperate, Janna's mother agreed to consult a psychic who was related to a friend. The seer asked to have a sealed paper bag holding some of Janna's possessions. Her "vision" of where Janna was wasn't encouraging. Gently, she said that Janna was no longer alive. Her earthly body was quite some distance from home.

"She's in a place with trees, a pond, and fallen logs," the woman said.

There were so many places like that in the Northwest where their family lived. Janna's mother began to feel that her missing daughter was trying her best to tell her something—maybe where to find her. Too many times for it to be someone with the wrong apartment number, there were knocks on her door at night. But when she opened it, there was no one there.

Once, in the most chilling phenomenon, a friend of the family named Linda was combing her hair, looking into a mirror in Janna's mother's apartment. As she looked at her own image, there was the sound of the familiar knock on the door. But this time, Linda became aware of another face in the mirror; someone was standing behind her, looking over her shoulder.

Linda had never met Janna, but she had seen her photographs. The other face in the mirror was Janna. She hovered there for a moment or two and then faded away. "I had the feeling," Linda said later, "that Janna was saying, 'Come and find me . . .'"

Twenty months after Janna disappeared, a member of a large commune, which was located about fifteen miles from where Janna had lived, was strolling through a wooded area when he saw a skull resting atop the earth at the base of a cherry tree.

The skull, which bore traces of cedar fronds and swamp cabbage, had come from a swampy area, had even been submerged in water perhaps, for a long time. But something or someone had brought it into the light and left it in the sunshine beneath the cherry tree.

By comparing dental records, forensic scientists confirmed that Janna had finally been found. There were no more knocks at her mother's door and no more floating faces in the mirrors.

The groundskeeper of the golf course where Janna vanished committed suicide when police approached him. Whether he was Janna's killer, no one knows. Even today, there are rumors that boys who were teenagers at the time carry some guilty knowledge of Janna's death. Time—as it always does—will tell.

The older I get, the more I wonder how big a part ghosts play in our lives. I try to judge less and wonder more.

In this book, my daughter Leslie writes about many cases that cannot be explained away by the realities that we tend to accept as proof. Some things simply cannot be proved, and must be taken on faith and with the knowledge that human beings know so little about life and death.

I don't know if I have influenced Leslie. When she was a very little girl, I used to read every book about hauntings that I could find in our small-town library. But I've never read anything as carefully researched as Leslie's books. She travels back in time (but not in any time machine) to get as close to the source of "ghost stories" as she can.

Our research techniques are quite similar; only the genres in which we write are different.

If you have ever wondered about things that cannot be scientifically proved, I think you will enjoy this book even more than *Coast to Coast Ghosts,* Leslie's first journey into the lives of people who came before us.

Acknowledgments

When it comes time to write the acknowledgments page, I always wish I had ten pages of space so I could put down the name of every person who was ever nice to me. My wonderful editor, Jennifer Fox, however, would probably frown upon it if I cut into the ghost stories to fill this book with thanks. So let me begin by saying that the people I am thanking here are currently in my life and they affect my day-to-day outlook. Please do not feel I have forgotten you if you do not find your name here. Others who deserve thanks are mentioned within the pages of this book, so consider yourself automatically acknowledged!

I've now done two books with my astute editor, Jennifer Fox, and I hope we will do many more together. I thank her for her enthusiasm, patience, and wise direction.

And, of course, I thank my agent, Sheree Bykofsky, who has proved she is a genius with words by not only authoring twelve books, but winning Scrabble championships and an impressive sum on TV's famous *Wheel of Fortune*.

I am so happy to have met the Scott family in 2002, the most creative family I know. Though most of them do not share my philosophies on ghosts, they have inspired me with their talent and friendship. Thanks to the whole Scott family and in particular Florence Scott, Glenn Scott, Dheb Gott, Luke Short, Jake Gott, Laurie Gott, Meridith Scott, and Vona Mae Scott.

Thanks to Ann Rule for passing along her writing genes and for being a continual source of support. And thank you to author Donna Anders, who is like an aunt to me!

During my travels to ghostly places, I've made a number of friends. Some have proved to be diligent researchers, diving into the mysteries that swirl around the ghost stories. Thanks to Katie Kizer and Alex Kizer for your research assistance. And thanks to Anita Dytuco and Amy Dytuco who not only scrutinized reels of newspaper microfilm but also chauffeured me around St. Louis and treated me like a queen.

Other people whose kind words and smiles have brought me gladness include Keitha L. Crain, Shirley Winkleman, Beth Winkleman, Martha Tuthill, Barbara Rike, Kathy Kraushar, Gregg Zehnder, Andy Zehnder, John Misura, John Knutzen, Doug and Sharon Bullis, Kelly McMurty, Tim King, Kevin Wagner, Celia Sadlou, Jim and Marge Toddle, Bill and Margarett Rudberg, Savanna Rudberg Schreiner, Lynn Rhone, Janice Owens, Andrea Owens, Phillip Owens, April Owens, Joseph Owens, Jeremy Owens, Kimberly Bruklis, Chrissanne Gordon, Neal and Nancy Fischer, Dr. Csaba Hegyvary, Jan Gill, Chuck Dwight, Earline Byers, and Harmonie Rose Keene.

My gratitude to Diana Rhodes and Michelle Johansson. I will always remember your extra dose of support!

And, as always, my thanks go to Marianne Burress, who has been in my corner rooting for me for thirty-seven years.

Introduction

They move silently among us. Sometimes we hear them—or *think* we do. A whisper. A giggle. A cough. In the next instant the sound is swallowed by the quiet and we are left to wonder if we only imagined it.

My friend Janice stopped by my house recently and when she rang the doorbell she heard the usual hysterical ruckus my dogs kick up whenever a visitor arrives. As she waited she heard a woman's voice soothe the animals. "*Shhh*. Quiet now. Quiet."

"The dogs quieted down," Janice told me. "But no one opened the door. That's when I knew it couldn't have been you I heard."

It certainly wasn't. Janice's teenage daughter, April, had been visiting me all morning and we had left half an hour earlier to walk to a nearby coffee shop.

"I knew you and April wouldn't just ignore me," said Janice. "I thought it could have been a ghost I heard. But I guess it could have been my imagination."

Maybe. Maybe not.

That's the way it often is with spirit encounters. They can be so faint and so fast that it is easy to dismiss them. Yet there are cases of those who not only hear ghosts clearly, but see them and interact with them. They, in fact, often do not suspect the "people" they are talking to are ethereal beings until they vanish before their eyes.

These are the stories that impress me the most—spirits appearing as seemingly solid human beings, so vivid and colorful there is no doubt they are real. The more witnesses, the better.

Yet ghosts may manifest as nothing more than an out-of-place shadow, a smoky shape swirling past, a tap on the shoulder, or a soft voice speaking a single word. Often just one person witnesses this type of paranormal event that is over so swiftly it is as if the universe hiccuped. Things were out of kilter for a fraction of a moment. The next moment, everything was normal again.

Perhaps you have had one of these encounters.

Perhaps you did and did not even notice.

Or maybe you are one of the lucky ones who actually got to see a fully materialized ghost.

Do you doubt there are ghosts among us?

If you do, that does not bother me one little bit. I simply hope you will be entertained by what I believe are true accounts of ghosts among us.

Fix yourself a cup of cocoa, find your favorite lap cat, sink into a comfortable chair, and be prepared to see some very interesting ghosts emerge in the following pages.

Oh, and if you feel someone breathing on the back of your neck, do not be alarmed. It is probably just a ghost reading over your shoulder.

Ghosts Among Us

Spirits of Seattle

Let me begin this book in the place it began for me. *Seattle.* And let me start as it started for me. It was a dark and stormy night . . .

Seriously.

I was born in the Virginia Mason Hospital on Seattle's haunted Capitol Hill. The night I made my entrance, the hospital lost its power in a storm. I was welcomed into the world by the wind moaning at the windows, and by the black, leafless trees that danced and creaked in the storm outside.

Technically, things actually began earlier with William Rule and Ann Stackhouse. It was at the haunted campus of the University of Washington where my parents met in creative writing class.

Certainly they were not thinking of me when their eyes met for the first time. They did not guess that they would be married and that their second daughter would grow up to be an author and write books about ghosts that included a chapter on that very campus.

But that is exactly what happened—though a few other things happened first.

On a spooky February night, I came into this world and would not stop screaming. As the doctors and nurses passed me around and tried to quiet me my mother reached out her arms and said, "Give her to me."

They did and I stopped crying immediately.

If you are one of the loyal readers of my mother's true-crime books (she has over twenty million books in print!), you might be saying, "Well, of course you stopped crying. It was Ann Rule, for God's sake."

I have to laugh at that because she wasn't a famous author then. She was a housewife and mother, whose lifelong dream of being a policewoman had been cut short when she was drummed off the force because of her poor vision.

This book is not really about me and my mother. But we will both play a minor role in some of the following stories. As those of you who read *Coast to Coast Ghosts* may recall, my mother is the woman who raised me in a haunted house.

To top that, she introduced me to a serial killer when I was fourteen. Of course she didn't know he was a killer at the time. The only ones who knew were his victims and they were gone. This tragic episode, too, will play a part in this book. If you are the impatient sort, you may skip ahead to chapter 15.

As for the rest of you, let me introduce you to haunted Seattle.

Phantoms of the Pike Place Public Market

She sat on her bed, her face pale and her lower lip trembling. "I saw her again today," she told me. "Did you see her?"

"No," I replied as I wondered what could be so frightening that it would have the seventeen-year-old girl shaking with fear.

"But you went to the market today," she said, and sounded almost angry as she demanded, "How could you not have seen her?"

"I don't know," I replied. "I looked for her, but I didn't see anyone who looked like that."

The terrified girl beside me had once again seen an unusual old woman at Pike Place Public Market—a woman she described as so evil that it scared her to talk about it.

It was the mid-1970s and we had no idea we were talking about a ghost—that the gnarled elderly woman she'd seen had been dead for a

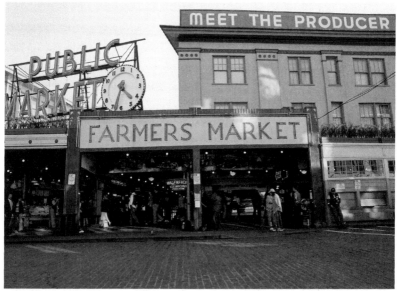

Seattle's Pike Place Public Market has had many years to gather ghosts. If you visit the market, study the crowd carefully, for some of the "people" you pass may be long dead. (Leslie Rule)

very long time. Twenty years would pass before I put two and two together and realized that she had seen a famous Seattle spirit.

I first learned the Pike Place Public Market was haunted when I began researching ghosts in 1995. I was poring over old articles at the Seattle Public Library when I stumbled across a story about ghosts at the market. When I read the description of one of the more frequently seen apparitions, I about fell off the chair.

It described the old woman who had frightened Belinda.* Though I rarely use a case where a witness won't let me use his or her name, I am including this one here, as I played a role in it. The person I'll call Belinda is very close to me and she has made me promise to never mention her in my writing. In fact, she is still so terrified by her experience at the market, she will not allow me to speak to her about it. Respecting her wishes, I will say only that she is a little older than I and that we saw each other daily during the 1970s.

---

* Whenever an asterisk appears, names have been changed to protect privacy.

The Pike Place Public Market overlooks Puget Sound in downtown Seattle. It is housed in an elongated structure with uneven floors and long corridors shooting off in all directions. It smells of fish, incense, and the indefinable scent of time past. The upper level is filled with farmers who peddle fresh produce and artists who showcase handmade wares such as leather belts, pottery, and stained-glass kaleidoscopes. The Pike Place Fish Market, famous because strong young men throw the fish to customers, dominates a corner. Street musicians are tucked into the alcoves and their music is ever present. Long ramps and wide staircases lead down to two lower levels where specialty and antiques shops are permanently housed.

When I was a teenager, the market was a hippie hangout and my friends and I went there to buy things like strobe candles, beaded earrings, and black light posters. My peers wore patchouli oil—a peculiar, sharp scent so popular among young people that the smell pervaded the market.

It was during this time that Belinda, our friends, and I often took the hour ride on the city bus to downtown Seattle, where we would hang out at the market or ride the ferryboats.

It was during her trips alone there that Belinda saw the old woman and described her as an Indian (a term that was not considered politically incorrect at the time) with sharp dark eyes that seemed to pierce Belinda's soul. She was an extremely old, toothless woman, who appeared to be a century old. Her shoulders were draped with a shabby shawl and her appearance was always accompanied by an overwhelming pungent odor of decay. During one encounter she spoke to Belinda, mumbling something incoherent.

"I think she's a witch!" Belinda told me. "It was like she was putting a spell on me!"

I looked for the old woman every time I strolled through the market. To my frustration—and Belinda's—I never saw her.

Belinda could not understand it. "She's always there," she said. "How could you *not* see her?"

I was perplexed. Extremely curious about the old woman, I had scrutinized every level of the market, searching for her. I wanted to see for myself what Belinda found so frightening.

Ghosts have been spotted on all of the levels of the Pike Place Public Market—including the lower floors where spirits swarm and sometimes make mischief. (Leslie Rule)

I now have the answer. The old woman was not a witch. She was a *ghost*. Over the years, many people have reported seeing her and say that they realized she was not of this world only when she evaporated before their eyes.

The consensus is that the ghost is that of Angeline, the daughter of "Chief" Sealth, for whom Seattle is named with a fractured spelling and pronunciation. Angeline lived in an unheated shack that was located where the market is now. She died in May 1896, an elderly woman of unknown age.

She became a favorite subject of a local photographer who paid her a dollar for each shot he took of her. Archival photographs show her digging for clams and laden with the handwoven baskets she peddled.

Evil? Nothing I've read indicates that Angeline Sealth was evil. When Belinda felt the sensation of evil it is possible that was simply a warning. As a result of their encounters, Belinda never returned to the market. Perhaps it was a dangerous place for her. We will never know.

Perhaps the feeling of evil came from the fact that Belinda was peering into "the other side." Some Christians, like Belinda, believe that ghost encounters are spiritually dangerous.

When it comes to the paranormal, no one has the answers and we must consider the possibility that Belinda *did* encounter something evil. Perhaps the apparition she saw was not Angeline but someone— or something—that we don't want to think about.

Is the ghost still there?

I recently gave a talk at a high school and I asked the kids if any of them had ever seen a ghost. A boy raised his hand and admitted he had seen something at the Pike Place Public Market. "It was an old Native American woman," he said, explaining that she vanished before his eyes.

When I told the kid that he was not the first to see the ghost, he appeared genuinely surprised. He had not heard that the Pike Place Public Market was haunted.

Opened in 1907, the market has had plenty of time to gather ghosts. In addition to Angeline, other apparitions seen there include a little blond boy who dashes past witnesses and a teenage boy of color.

Who are they?

I've yet to identify the source for the little boy, but wonder if the teenager could be a sailor who died at the market in the 1940s. A retired detective remembered the incident. "That area was my beat," he told me. "A sailor was walking on a sky bridge there and fell to his death." No one knew if the sailor's death was an accident. The sky bridge was later removed in a remodel. The same detective remembered an eccentric market security guard who was also found dead there after a fall. The guard was notorious for climbing over walls and taking risky shortcuts. "You never knew when he would come popping over a wall," the detective remembered.

Perhaps he is still patrolling the Pike Place Public Market, keeping the other ghosts in line.

More Market Ghosts

Sheila Lyon, co-owner of the Market Magic Shop for decades, has the inside scoop on the ethereal beings who roam the market. Fellow shop owners have shared so many of their ghostly encounters with her that she now runs the Haunted Market Ghost Tour, which she gives weekly from October through May.

According to Sheila, the owner of the market's Bead Shop was long plagued by two ghosts seen frequently in the store—a Native American woman and a little blond boy. "She hired a shaman to release their spirits," said Sheila. The paranormal activity immediately ceased at the Bead Shop, but the spirits apparently didn't travel far, for odd things began to happen at the Wisdom Marionette store. "The owners would come in in the morning and find the marionettes moved around as if someone had been playing with them," she said, explaining that the activity continued until the shop moved.

Sheila says that other paranormal phenomena at the market include:
- A pole that is icy cold no matter how hot the day.
- Frequent reports of an eerie lullaby, echoing throughout the market. It is believed to be the ghost of "the fat lady barber" who worked there years ago and was notorious for lulling her patrons to sleep with her singing so she could pick their pockets.
- Sightings of a dapper dancing man, who wears a double-breasted suit, that go back to the World War II era. "The ladies who worked the swing shift at Boeing used to go to the 'Dime a Dance' at the market after work," said Sheila. "I've spoken to three different women who remember dancing with the ghost and they all describe him the same way."

For information on the Haunted Market Ghost Tour, e-mail Sheila Lyon at sheila@speakeasy.net.

More Seattle Ghosts

Legendary among locals as a haunted house, the Georgetown Castle looks the part. The 1889 turreted stone home in Georgetown in the outskirts of Seattle wears the years with a spooky apathy. Over the last several decades, the private residence's stories have been presented on TV and in Seattle newspapers with occupants quoted on a most disturbing encounter.

Witnesses insist they've seen the ghost of a tall old woman in a long white dress who chokes herself as her eyes burn with horror. Legend says she is the granddaughter of the house's builder and lost her mind when her baby was killed. The story goes that the child was born out of wedlock and that her lover murdered it and buried it beneath the back porch.

The ghost of a woman in a raincoat is reportedly seen at the University of Washington's Suzzallo Library. While some say that the ghost story is a hoax, others insist that the tall, slender apparition appears at closing time and is seen headed toward the stacks. When library employees follow her to let her know the library is closing, she is nowhere to be found. All that is left is the hollow sound of her footsteps hitting the floor. The sound grows fainter as if she is walking away.

The Harvard Exit Theatre on Capitol Hill is thought to be the home of the ghost of the Emerald City's first mayor, Bertha Landes. Elected in 1926 at age fifty-seven, Mayor Landes is remembered for her successful fight of corruption in Seattle. Over the years numerous witnesses have reported seeing the apparition of a woman dressed in 1920s fashion, who floats several feet above the floor. Some report the ghost disappears into walls.

Many assume the spirit belongs to the former mayor because she was a member of the Woman's Century Club, the first organization to occupy the brick building. The Harvard Exit Theatre is popular for the artsy and independent films shown there, as well as for the spectacular lobby. The grand piano, sparkling chandelier, and 1920s decor may very well beckon to a spirit from that era.

HARVARD EXIT THEATRE
807 EAST ROY AT HARVARD
SEATTLE, WA 98102
(206) 781-5755

Playtime

Ask any baby boomer who grew up with TV about "Talking Tina" and you are sure to see a shudder. *The Twilight Zone* was a program ahead of its time with thirty-minute tales of macabre twists on reality.

Never mind that the eerie episodes were filmed in shades of gray and viewed on tiny TV screens. The ingenious plots, superb scripts, and exquisite directing and acting coaxed the imagination to life. The words of a wide-eyed doll are etched forever on the memories of millions of *Twilight Zone* fans: "My name is Talking Tina and I'm going to kill you."

Long before Chucky (the movie doll who is possessed by a serial killer), the 1960s "Talking Tina" episode terrified America's children. How many little girls banished a favorite doll from a place of honor on their beds to the bottom of the toy chest? (Thank you, Rod Serling.)

But toys don't *really* come to life. That's just pretend, right?

Wrong.

While I hope to never find a case of a murderous doll, my files are fat with cases of toys that seem to have minds of their own. These toys, of course, aren't really thinking, conscious beings. They are, more likely, simply objects that are haunted. Many of these toys have been exposed to dramatic human emotion and have soaked up this energy like a sponge soaking up spilled milk. In some cases, the toys may not be the source of a haunting but are objects of interest to ghosts.

Mama's Little Helper

Rhonda Lillie stirred in her sleep. As she awoke, the dark filled her eyes. It was 3 A.M. and she'd been snoozing soundly in the Oxnard, California, rental home she shared with her husband and two daughters. *What is that?* she wondered as she sat up and strained to make sense of an odd tinkling sound.

"Wake up!" She nudged her husband. "I hear something." He pulled the pillow over his head and ignored her.

Rhonda got out of bed and headed down the hallway, past the rooms where her children slept as she moved toward the noise. The dust of her dreams had cleared. Alert now, she could identify the sound. It was her children's electronic toy—a ball that sings whenever it is played with. "I knew my kids were asleep," said Rhonda. "The ball makes noise only when it is touched."

Yet Rhonda wasn't frightened. She opened the door to the playroom, flicked on the light, and saw the ball wiggling and "singing" in the middle of the room. A shrill siren sounded near her ear and she turned to see a toy police car on the dresser. The little blue light atop its roof blinked as the car moved forward on the dresser. But before it reached the edge, it backed up and then moved forward again.

It repeated the action, each time stopping before it reached the edge of the dresser. It was as if an invisible hand guided it, stopping it just before it crashed to the floor.

"You don't have to do this," Rhonda spoke calmly to the empty room. "I know you are here." She turned off the toys and went back to bed.

Rhonda does not believe the toys themselves were haunted. They were simply playthings for an ethereal little girl who shared their old white stucco house. While some people might have been disturbed by the 3 A.M. wake-up call, Rhonda took it in stride. In fact, she would not have had it any other way.

"I'll always be grateful to her," confided Rhonda, who first became aware her family was not alone one summer afternoon when she was in the bathroom. "The door was open, and I glanced up just as a ball flew past. A second later a little girl rushed by, chasing after it."

"Hey!" Rhonda shouted. "Don't throw the ball in the house." She figured it was her daughter, but when she entered the hallway, it was quiet. "Angel!" she called out to her four-year-old. When there was no answer, Rhonda went outside, where she found Angel happily splashing alone in the plastic wading pool.

"But, Mom!" Angel protested as Rhonda reprimanded her. "I wasn't in the house!"

One day soon after, Rhonda was doing housework when she heard Angel chattering away in her bedroom as if she were involved in an animated conversation.

"Who were you talking to?" Rhonda later asked her daughter.

"I was playing with the girl," Angel replied.

Rhonda smiled. "At first I thought she had an imaginary friend," she explained. But Angel was so adamant, her mother found herself wondering, *Could she have met the ghost too?*

According to Angel, her friend was definitely not imaginary. Today, at thirteen, she vividly recalls her play session with a most unusual little girl nine years before. "I looked into my room and saw her playing with my things," said Angel. "At first I was mad and then I decided she'd be fun to play with."

She stared for a moment at the strange figure. "She was glowing and blue," said Angel. "She was a Hispanic girl about six, with long hair that fell to her waist."

Angel sat down beside the child, who was clutching Angel's teddy bear. "She kept staring at me. She looked kind of strange. She had squinty eyes, as if she was crying. Her hair looked damp. Every once in a while she'd laugh. But she would not say a word."

Though a bit apprehensive about her odd playmate, Angel was glad to have someone to play with. There were no other children in the neighborhood and she was lonely. "But I knew she wasn't like normal people," remembered Angel.

When Angel tried to take her teddy bear back, the glowing girl clutched it tightly, refusing to give it up.

The play session ended when the strange child tossed the teddy bear across the room. "I went to get it and when I looked back, she was gone."

She saw the girl again a few days later when she awoke shivering from a sound sleep. "I was so cold it woke me up. I looked up and there was the little girl staring down at me. It frightened me. She looked so sad."

A year passed and it was summertime once again when the ghost girl made another appearance. "Angel was playing in the wading pool, and I stood at the kitchen sink watching her as I did the dishes," remembered Rhonda. My one-year-old, Amanda, was just out of sight of the window when I heard a voice in my head."

It was more than a thought. It was as if someone were speaking to her, yet the voice did not ring in her ears. The warning was louder than any spoken word.

The baby is choking.

In that instant, she saw the little ghost at the edge of her vision. "She was about six with long brown hair and she was wearing a white dress."

Rhonda whirled around and the girl vanished.

She rushed outside to find Amanda sitting on the ground, her face red, and her mouth filled with dirt. Frantically, Rhonda reached into the choking baby's mouth and pulled out a huge dirt clod. "She was okay," said the grateful mother. "But if a few more seconds had passed, she might not have been!"

(Left to right) Amanda, Angel, Rhonda, and Ashley all get goose bumps when they talk about the sad little ghost who once played at the Lillie home. (Leslie Rule)

𝔊𝔥𝔬𝔰𝔱𝔰 𝔦𝔫 𝔱𝔥𝔢 𝔑𝔢𝔴𝔰

The Haunted Swing Set

GHOSTLY KIDS PLAYING ROUGH? It seems some mischievous spirits are having a little too much fun with the kids at a Pocatello park.

The *Pocatello (Idaho) State Journal* reported that Ammon Park was the site of an investigation of odd activity. The October 2003 article said that the probe by the Ghosts of Idaho (GOI) team had prompted reports of paranormal experiences at the park.

One former Pocatello resident remembered a terrifying incident years earlier when she and a playmate entered a utility shed on a summer day. Though the children were alone in the park, the door slammed shut and was latched from the outside, locking them inside.

The recent exploration of the park began because of a tip given to investigator Tracy Eastman. A witness told Eastman that when he was a boy, in 1992, he was playing in the park with some friends. They were sitting beneath a pine tree when they heard a noise. The boys looked up to see a little girl in a blue dress seated on the swing. As the stunned boys watched her swing, she suddenly vanished. The boys silently jumped to their feet and took off running as ghostly giggling rang out behind them.

In a recent experiment, Chris Elder of GOI set up a video camera and taped the swing set and discovered that one of the four swings "was moving rapidly while the others were moving slowly."

The investigators were unable to locate any documentation of a girl dying in the park and surmised that the giggling ghost girl may have once lived in the area and played in the park.

Rhonda's family has moved several times since they lived in the Oxnard house. But the place has left a strong impression on them all. "In addition to the little girl, my sister and I also saw an old Hispanic man in a big hat," said Rhonda. "We often heard strange noises and the lights would turn themselves on and off."

Amanda, the baby saved from choking, also remembered an experience in the home. Ten years old now, Amanda recalled the night she woke to see a little girl curled up sleeping on the floor beside her bed. "I thought it was Angel," she said. "But Angel was asleep in the bed!"

Perhaps it was the same little spirit who had once saved her life. Perhaps she was still watching over her.

Who were the ghostly people who shared the Lillies' home?

"They may have been fieldworkers," ventured Rhonda. "Before the house was built, there was a farm there."

Why was the little girl so sad? Why was she seen in the summertime? Twice she showed up while Angel played in the wading pool.

Angel remembered that the ghost girl had wet hair. Was the ghost child a drowning victim?

Though these questions remain unanswered, one thing is certain. The spirit girl meant no harm. "She saved Amanda's life," said Rhonda. "For that, we will always be thankful."

Bakery Boy

Author Troy Taylor leased an old building in Alton, Illinois, and found it perfect for his bookstore. Troy is in the ghost business. He's written over a dozen books on hauntings and he runs Alton's History and Hauntings Ghost Tours.

The 1857 building with its creaky wood floors and spacious rooms was exactly what he had in mind. But when the owners told him the building was haunted, he secretly scoffed.

"It was *too* perfect," he said.

"The building is haunted by a little boy whose father worked here years ago when it was a bakery," Troy was told.

The declaration smacked of a salesman's line, custom fit for him.

He and his wife, Amy, brushed the story aside and got to work setting up their business. "We forgot all about it," admitted Troy.

Before long employees began reporting odd things. "They heard whispering and footsteps after the store closed," he explained.

One afternoon as Troy worked in the store he was at the counter engrossed in paperwork when he felt "one of my children tug on the back of my sweatshirt. It was several sharp tugs. I turned to see what my child wanted and was startled to realize that no one was there."

In fact, Troy was all alone in the shop.

The paranormal activity escalated in the following months. Objects inexplicably vanished, only to pop up in unexpected places days later. "Then he followed us home," said Troy.

When Amy and Troy welcomed their new baby girl, Maggie, everyone was enchanted with the dimpled red-haired child—everyone including an unseen presence.

"The most chilling incident occurred when Maggie was about three months old," Troy remembered. "She was in her crib asleep and started to cry around two A.M."

The alert parents heard the crying via the baby monitor and had jumped out of bed when they heard *another* sound—the "faint tinkle of music."

Concerned, they rushed to check on their child. "She was lying quietly, watching the mobile above her crib going around, playing music as it turned."

Troy shook his head, bemused by the occurrence. The infant, of course, was too tiny to have activated the mobile. "Someone had actually wound it up completely in order for it to have started playing," explained Troy. "It had not been triggered on its own because we had never used it.

"As the baby got bigger, she was able to sit by herself in the living room and play. We noticed an interesting phenomenon. Toys vanished and operated by themselves."

The enigmatic presence seemed to have his favorite toys. These would vanish regularly. "We'd leave toys on the rug when we took the baby into the next room to eat dinner, and when we'd return they'd be

Troy Taylor in his haunted bookstore where the ghost of a little boy makes mischief. (Leslie Rule)

gone. They always came back later—often after a day or two—and always appeared in spots we had already searched.

"We have an ongoing problem with toys that turn themselves on. It happens at all hours of the day and night."

One evening as Troy watched television, he noticed Mollie, his big orange cat, staring at one of the baby's toys. "It is a tall pole with a circle on top that plastic balls can be placed inside of. When the ball is pushed down into a slot, music plays and the ball whirls around and shoots out the bottom."

Mollie crouched, her pupils huge, as if watching an invisible prey. "I suddenly heard music and the whirring of a ball!" Troy exclaimed.

Mollie's fur stood up and she dashed to the other room. "I was startled too," said Troy. "Someone would have to pick up the ball and place it in the opening to start it working. *I* didn't do it. The *cat* couldn't do it. It had to be our little resident ghost."

Today Troy puts more credence in the stories of the child who once spent his days in the building. "They say when it was a bakery, the boy's father worked there," Troy said, explaining that the boy accompanied his baker dad to work early in the morning. As the sweet, heavy scent of baking bread wafted through the shop, the child would play or sleep on a cot in the back of the shop. The boy died young but his spirit never left the premises—until he was enticed by a beautiful baby girl.

Tess, the Haunted Doll

Kelly Weaver of Camp Hill, Pennsylvania, did not know why she purchased the odd doll at a yard sale. "I am *not* a doll person," insists the aspiring writer. "But there was something about her face that kept drawing me to her. I couldn't put her down."

So she plunked down the dollar for the small plastic doll and took her home. "She was dressed in Russian garb. She wore an orange and brown floral skirt—which I thought was ugly. Her arms were folded across her chest."

The blonde, rosy-cheeked doll smiled prettily and Kelly found herself talking to her as she climbed into the car beside her husband,

John. Even as she did so, Kelly laughed at herself. "Can you believe it?" she said to John. "I'm too old to play with dolls—and here I am *talking* to one!"

He smiled patiently. "You're never too old for dolls. Just enjoy it!" he replied.

Kelly, who has always had a strong sixth sense, confided, "In my mind, I 'heard' the doll tell me her name was Tess."

Imagination or psychic impression? It didn't matter. From that moment on, the doll was Tess.

The next day Kelly set up her computer on a picnic table and began writing a novel. She propped Tess beside the computer for inspiration. Inspire her she did! "The words flowed and I liked what I wrote. Whenever I touched her, I felt surges of energy."

Kelly named a character after the charismatic doll.

Her friends, too, noticed Tess had an aliveness about her foreign to an inanimate object. "Her eyes seemed to follow you!" said Kelly.

An antiques dealer friend informed her that Tess was an old-fashioned tea cozy. Her skirt was designed to cover a teapot. This struck Kelly as odd because she had just rewritten a chapter after being inexplicably compelled to add a tea party scene.

All of this, of course, could be nothing more than imagination and coincidence. Yet who can explain what happened next?

"I was reading my work to John while he was lying in bed. He asked me where Tess was. I pointed to the top of the television, which is set up high atop a trunk."

John fell asleep, but Kelly was restless, so she went to another room to read. When she was finally sleepy, she crawled into bed. She snuggled into the pillow only to see familiar eyes staring back at her. *Tess!* The doll was on the pillow beside her, yet Kelly had not placed her there.

How did she get there?

John was bewildered by the occurrence.

"When I woke Kelly I asked her why she was sleeping with the doll. She said she had not put her there."

Could the dog, Teddy, have retrieved the doll and tucked it in beside his mistress?

John shook his head. "I am fundamentally a skeptic. I try to explore every rational explanation for something strange before I accept it as being paranormal or supernatural. Any attempt by Teddy to fetch the doll would have caused a major commotion," he said, explaining that two stacks of boxes flank the trunk and TV where Tess rested. "It would have been physically impossible for Teddy to climb up and retrieve the doll without knocking down a large number of items, and everything was intact."

John, still searching for a logical explanation, asked, "Could Kelly, in a sleepwalking state, have done it unconsciously?"

He dismissed the idea as soon as he raised it. "I've never known her to sleepwalk and there is nothing to suggest she does."

The Tess incident paints a spooky picture. Imagine the little doll, her skirt swishing as she hops down from her high place and skitters across the room. . . .

Or did she float through the air as unseen hands carried her? Perhaps she vanished from atop the TV and promptly materialized beside Kelly.

If the dog witnessed this, he is definitely not talking.

Clowning Around

When Renee walked into her spare room to pick up a basket of dirty laundry, she gasped. Her clown doll was propped up in front of the basket, staring at her with his wide brown eyes. "He'd been in the corner for several months," said the Beaverton, Oregon, real estate agent. "I hadn't moved him."

She quizzed her boyfriend, Mark, and her seventeen-year-old daughter and neither of them had moved the doll. She was a little spooked but not surprised. She had, in fact, gotten exactly what she'd shopped for—a haunted clown doll!

She had been surfing the Internet, reading ghost stories, when she entered the word "haunted" into "Search."

"An eBay auction came up," said Renee. "It was about to end in four minutes."

Those with computers hooked to the Internet can access eBay, an online auction site where people can bid on or sell everything from Avon bottles to automobiles. The bidding was in the hundreds for the

Vincent Hitchcock, the haunted clown doll, poses on a dock outside of a Portland, Oregon, restaurant. The enigmatic doll sometimes moves on his own. (Leslie Rule)

clown doll with the big rubber head, round nose, and straw-stuffed body. The main selling point? It was *haunted!*

The doll, the seller claimed, moved on its own.

Renee, who asked that her last name be left out of this story, has always been interested in ghosts. "I grew up in Walla Walla, Washington," she said. "My friends lived in an 1800s house that was haunted and I used to spend the night there. We would hear chains rattling and a woman screaming at night." So began her fascination with "the other side."

As she stared at the photograph of the unusual-looking doll with the mysterious habits, she made a decision. On a whim, Renee entered a bid. Moments later, she received an e-mail telling her that she had won! For about five hundred dollars the doll was hers. Suddenly, she felt nervous.

"I didn't want it to come to my house," she confided. "So I went and got a post office box and had the seller mail it to me there."

Once she opened the package, the doll seemed innocent enough, so she brought him home. He looked to be many decades old, but there were no dates or other markings on him. His clothing was 1960s vintage, but Renee could not tell if it was his original attire. "We named him Vincent Hitchcock," she said, explaining that he was named after two eerie cinema icons—monster-movie actor Vincent Price and suspense-film director Alfred Hitchcock.

She corresponded with the seller, who told her that he was a doll sculptor and that he, too, had purchased the clown doll on eBay. He, however, had no idea that the doll came with a ghost. He simply wanted it because it had such an interesting face. But he soon began to notice that the clown would mysteriously vanish from the places he left him only to show up in unexpected spots.

"He contacted the previous owner," said Renee. "He asked him if there was something unusual about the doll. The guy told him, 'Yeah! He *moves!*'"

That man's wife made him put the clown in the shed.

Renee, however, has a place of honor in her home for Vincent. She also has a Web site on ghosts with a section devoted to Vincent's activities. Since he has shared her home, he has inexplicably moved several times. Once they found him with his arm up in the air.

Renee has also experimented with electronic voice phenomena (EVP), the practice of leaving a tape recorder running in an empty room in the hope of capturing spirit voices on tape. Left beside Vincent, the recorder has gotten several phrases, spoken in the gravelly voice of a man, which can be heard on her Web site.

In the clearest recording, the voice yells, "Wake up!"

After capturing the phrase, Renee played the recording for her daughter, who turned white. "She said she'd heard the voice in the night and it had woken her up."

Where in the world did Vincent come from? He may have been homemade, perhaps for a poor child, Renee thinks, with a rubber head purchased from a craft shop.

All who meet Vincent agree that there is a childlike aura about him.

If a spirit is indeed attached to the clown, it may be a child or someone with childlike energy.

Despite Renee's research into Vincent's "life," his past and the ghost that came with him remain a mystery.

The World's Most Famous Haunted Toy Store

Sunnyvale, California, holds a place on the map as the location of the most famous haunted toy store in the world. Shoppers and employees alike have reported experiencing paranormal activity there. Witnesses have seen toys hop off shelves, spotted apparitions, and heard a voice calling, "Elizabeth."

The store's restrooms are a hot spot of activity where some say that the faucets turn themselves off and toilets flush by themselves.

A famous psychic claims that the ghost of a man named Johnny was chopping wood and accidentally cut himself on the spot years ago before the store was built. He supposedly bled to death and his ghost remains today.

three

Haunted Amusement Parks

What is it that is so especially creepy about a haunted amusement park?

Perhaps it is the fact that these places are supposed to be about fun and laughter—places where young romance blossoms in the "tunnel of love" and where families enjoy caramel apples and big wads of pink cotton candy and make happy memories on the merry-go-round.

The thrills at amusement parks are supposed to be just that. Thrills. Yes, youngsters like to be scared silly on rides, but they don't expect to actually *die*.

The International Association of Amusement Parks and Attractions recently reported that the chances of being killed on a ride are 1 in 760 million. Statistically, folks are safer on a roller coaster than driving on the freeway. Yet with the millions of people who indulge in thrill rides, the rare mishaps do occur.

Tragically, disaster eventually strikes almost every amusement park. The odds are that you will have a great time and leave intact. Yet not everyone does. Accidents happen and some thrill seekers *never* leave. Oh, their bodies may be ferried away and laid to rest, but their spirits remain behind where they sometimes give unexpected thrills and chills to others who are just like they used to be. *Alive.*

It's a Scream!

It was dusk on a cold October evening in the year 2000 in Conneaut Lake, Pennsylvania, as Bonnie and Regis Easler waited for the last guest of the season. As managers of Conneaut Lake Park's historic Hotel Conneaut, it was their job to tuck the rustic old building in for the frigid winter ahead. A chill wind blew off the lake and dark clouds smoldered in the sky. A storm was coming.

The nearby rides had stopped twirling, churning, and rolling. The excited shrieks of the passengers had faded with the summer, and the scent of cotton candy was now a sweet memory. The amusement park was empty and the icy fingers of winter were creeping in.

Bonnie shivered and stepped inside. She was in the lobby when she heard music. "We don't have TVs or radios in the rooms," she told me. "So I figured the guest must have arrived and brought his own radio."

She headed down the hall toward the music. As she got closer, she recognized the tune as an old-time waltz and it was coming from the ballroom. The huge sliding door to the ballroom was slightly ajar, so Bonnie peered in. She was stunned to see a couple dancing. "They wore old-fashioned clothes," she said. "The man's suit had tails and the woman wore a gown and her hair flew out behind her." The apparitions' profiles were sharp and clear, yet they were as colorless as an autumn mist.

Restless spirits roam the grounds of the Hotel Conneaut. (Leslie Rule)

The Hotel Conneaut deck looks out over the lake. If you visit, enjoy the view, but beware—someone could be looking over your shoulder. (Leslie Rule)

Curious, Bonnie slid open the door for a better look. "The door made a big clunking noise," she said. And with the sound, the scene ended. The couple dissipated like two puffs of smoke in a breeze.

Bonnie was both shaken and excited. In her many years at the hotel, she had heard stories about the ghosts there but until now had never seen one.

Moments later, she had yet *another* paranormal experience. "I was outside with my husband and a friend and I noticed that a second-floor window was open."

"The bed will get soaked," she commented as raindrops started to spatter around them. The friend had never seen the rooms, so the three trooped upstairs. Bonnie slid the window down and locked it. Back outside, they looked up and saw that the window was wide open, its curtain flapping in the wind. "Our friend left and refused to come back!" said Bonnie.

Western Pennsylvania's Conneaut Lake Park was once *the* destination for excitement-seeking travelers. It opened in 1892 as Exposition Park. About thirty-five miles west of Erie, the hub of activity was *more* than a park. It was a *city*. Visitors could arrive by train from a number of places and had their choice of over a dozen hotels within the park.

Decades later, great luminaries of the time such as Doris Day and Perry Como (who was once a barber there) sang to excited audiences in the park's Beach Club.

Today the park is rich with charm, but poor on the funds needed to run it. It is owned by the community; volunteers are scrambling to save it from demolition. Conneaut Lake Park and its remaining hotel are favorite places of those who visit for the nostalgia and some who visit for the *ghosts*!

Bonnie is just one of many who have experienced ghosts at the Conneaut Lake Park. In fact, others have described the exact same scenario of the dancing couple in the ballroom. In addition to seeing apparitions at the hotel, people have witnessed objects floating in midair and heard phantom footsteps and crying.

Dozens say they have seen the specter of Elizabeth, and area people are aware of her legend. The story goes that she was a lovely woman whose wedding took place at the hotel. On her wedding night (or sometimes on the night *before* the wedding, depending on who is telling the story) a fire ravaged the hotel and poor Elizabeth was trapped. Her husband escaped harm but his bride perished.

Archive searches have yet to validate this, though the park has suffered fires, including one in 1908 that gutted a major part of the midway and destroyed four hotels within the park. The Hotel Conneaut lost 150 rooms in an April 1943 fire. Was there a bride killed in that fire? Or was that story born out of imagination? Perhaps concocted to explain the many sightings of the ghostly woman who wanders the hotel's halls?

Hotel management points to countless reports from guests and employees who have spotted the ethereal lady. Some say she steps out of the wall that once opened to a hallway in the part of the hotel that burned. Clad in 1940s clothing, she glances around as if lost before she vanishes.

Perhaps there really *was* an Elizabeth. No matter her name, witnesses insist a ghostly lady haunts the halls of the Hotel Conneaut.

Friction in the Kitchen

The Hotel Conneaut's downstairs restaurant, Steak on the Lake, is home to the ghosts of two chefs who have been seen frequently over the years. Witnesses have reported a spooky scenario played out in the kitchen. The scene, they say, materializes before their eyes as two men in chef uniforms fight, tossing pots and pans and knives at each other.

During my visit, I was walking up the stairs when I met a group of young women who were coming down and we began talking. When the conversation turned to ghosts, they shared a startling encounter they had had weeks before on one of their frequent stays at the hotel. Liza Shaftic, seventeen, Jennifer Hamett, twenty, Larissa Stefano, nineteen, and Nikki Jo Piccirillo, eighteen, all from New Castle, Pennsylvania, had been out late on a July night in 2003. They returned at about three in the morning and entered through the hotel's backdoor, which took them past the closed restaurant. They glanced through the window and saw a chef. "We all stood there and just stared at him as he stared back," said Liza, shivering at the memory. "He was sitting at a table next to the hostess stand right through the main doors of the dining room. He looked as if he was writing on a piece of paper."

Left to right: Liza Shaftic, Larissa Stefano, and Jen Hamett on the pier outside the Hotel Conneaut. They were terrified when they encountered a ghost at the hotel. (Leslie Rule)

There was something about his penetrating stare that chilled them. His eyes seemed to bore into them. "After a moment, we realized what we were actually seeing," said Liza. The four stood frozen until, all at once, it hit them that he was not of this world. "We all ran up the steps toward the front desk of the hotel, and straight to our room. The next night, we told the desk clerk and two security guards about what we had seen."

The girls were startled to learn they were not the first to see the ghost of a chef. "We knew the hotel was haunted, but it was the first we heard about a chef," said Larissa.

On the night they saw the chef, the restaurant had been closed since 9 P.M. Employees had locked up hours before. "The security guards told us that they found a broken window in the restaurant the night we saw the ghost," said Jennifer.

Was the mysterious man simply an intruder? That, of course, would be the most logical explanation if not for the fact the man they saw was dressed in a vintage chef uniform—complete with a bow tied up at his neck. The girls were insistent about that fact.

As I loaded up a plate in the buffet line during dinner the next night, I noticed the restaurant manager rushing by and stopped him to tell him about the girls' sighting. "Do your chefs wear uniforms like that?" I asked.

"No, our chefs don't wear ties," he replied. "And no one is *ever* here that late."

Hotel security validated the girls' story. They had indeed reported seeing a man in the restaurant the same night the window was broken.

What was the phantom chef writing on that piece of paper? His secret recipe? A suicide note? Since the frightened girls were in too much of a hurry to stop and read, it will remain an enigma.

Ups and Downs

Click, click, click, click, click. It makes a sound like a stick running over a picket fence. The rhythm is slow at first, and then so fast that it vanishes beneath the shrieks and screams. It is the "song" of the Blue Streak Roller Coaster. Since 1938 the rhythmic click of the coaster cars rolling over the wooden slats has been "music" as familiar to Conneaut Lake Park visitors as the sweet scent of cotton candy permeating the air.

The Blue Streak Roller Coaster, a vintage wooden relic that thrills today just as it did in years past, may give riders more than they bargained for. This writer normally avoids fast and furious white-knuckle rides, but for the sake of research I huddled into a car, held on tight, and managed to live through the sharp climbs and terrifying plunges. Though *I* managed to live, not everyone has.

A park historian, who was born and raised nearby, remembered the tragedy on the Blue Streak in the 1940s. "It was during the war," he recalled. "A drunken sailor stood up during a hairpin turn and was thrown out and killed."

A huge clown head grins above the entry to Kiddieland at Conneaut Lake Park. Phantom horses are heard galloping through this section of the park. (Leslie Rule)

The sharp turn, he explained, was later softened into a more gentle curve to prevent future accidents.

Does the sailor haunt the Blue Streak? Maybe so, but I've found no one who has seen his ghost. A Blue Streak ride operator, however, confided he *has* seen a ghost there. A ride was just ending, and the empty cars were shooting toward him so he could load them up with eager passengers. "The roller coaster malfunctioned," he told me, describing how instead of stopping, an empty car shot past him and disappeared into the "Skunk Tunnel." The young man went to retrieve it and the moment he entered the dark tunnel he felt his heart leap into his throat. There, in the middle of the tracks, was a little glowing girl. "She was in front of the car," he said. "She had a long dress on that came to here." He touched his mid-calf and added, "I've never gone back into the tunnel since." He shuddered. "I refuse to do it."

This Blue Streak Roller Coaster operator was shocked to see something unexpected in the tunnel. (Leslie Rule)

Who was the ghostly child? Did she die on the roller coaster? No records of her have been found. Is she a child who died nearby? She could have lived in one of the homes inside the amusement park. Maybe the excited energy of children riding the roller coaster attracted her to it.

If you visit Conneaut Lake Park and ride the Blue Streak, make sure you keep your eyes open in the tunnel. Perhaps you, too, will see the little girl ghost.

More Conneaut Ghost Stories

Front desk clerk and college student Carrie Pavlik was so fascinated with the ghosts of Conneaut Lake Park that she compiled anecdotes from guests and fellow employees and recently printed them in a seventy-one-page booklet. The chilling stories she collected include the following ghostly encounters:

- An employee unlocked the kitchen in the Steak on the Lake restaurant one morning and discovered all the brooms and garbage cans mysteriously lined up in the center of the room.
- A soldier sitting in a tree beside the hotel has been seen countless times.
- A guest was tripped on the hotel stairs by a little girl on a tricycle. Legend has it the child had a fatal accident on those steps while riding her tricycle.
- Guests have awoken to find a "man" rummaging through their things. Before they can confront him, he vanishes before their eyes.
- The phantom trotting of horses' hooves is frequently heard in the park's Kiddieland.
- A gold wedding band once materialized in the change slot of the hotel pay phone. Some say the ring belonged to the ghost of Elizabeth, who died there on her wedding night.

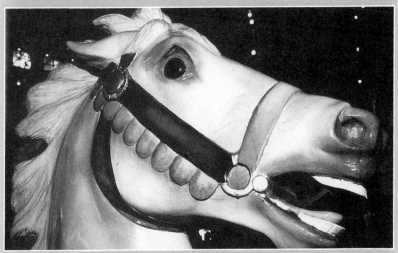

This carousel horse at Conneaut Lake Park mirrors the spooked expression of some visitors when they encounter something strange there. (Leslie Rule)

More Thrill Rides

Mad Man

The Six Flags over Texas in Arlington is said to be home to many ghosts. Rob Lockhart, who worked there in the 1970s, has never forgotten the excitement among the employees about the ghost sightings. Riders of the LaSalle Riverboat Ride got a thrill they hadn't bargained for when they spotted the specter of a nude old man swimming in the river. He was seen so frequently he was dubbed "the Mad Man of the Lavacca."

"Every time a swamp rat—that's what we called the river ride employees—would report seeing the old man in the water, security investigated," Rob remembered. "They never found anything. The ride was located in the center of the park and it would have been very hard for anyone to sneak in and take a dip in the water."

According to Rob, another haunting at the park is connected to a man who fell to his death while doing roofing work on the Southern Palace, which was once an amphitheater. "He haunts the theater," said Rob. Doors open and shut by themselves and toilets flush when no one has touched them.

Shattered Grave

Largo, Maryland, is legendary as the site of the haunted Six Flags America, previously known as Adventure World. Some say that the apparition of a child in white has spooked employees there for years. She is rumored to be buried in an old family graveyard on the site. The grave of "Elinor" was marked with a stone that was broken when a bulldozer ran over it and some think she has been restless ever since.

Peek-a-Boo

Paramount's King's Island in Cincinnati, Ohio, has had just a little over three decades to gather ghosts, but it has managed to muster up a few, according to local legend. A blonde girl wearing a blue dress is said to play in the Waterworks, where she startles employees after closing. Just like Elinor in Largo, this ghost is rumored to be that of a child buried there. Her graveyard is supposedly between the parking lot and the campground. Other ghosts there are believed to be people who allegedly died on the Beast and the Octopus.

Scary-Go-Rounds

Historic merry-go-rounds are hauntingly beautiful. Add a ghost or two and they are still beautiful yet even *more* haunting.

The Lonely Ride

It was the early 1980s when Mike Ball took his four young daughters to ride the carousel in Portland, Oregon, at the Jantzen Beach Mall. Ages two through ten, his girls were well behaved as they waited in line for their turn to mount a majestic animal aboard the historic carousel. Two other children, however, were *not* so well behaved. In fact, they were so naughty that Mike found himself getting annoyed as he watched them playing aboard the merry-go-round. "I thought they were the children of the operator," remembered the letter carrier, who lives in Portland with his wife, Pat. "They were unruly, but she didn't pay any attention to them. They were running around in the middle of the carousel, in the machinery," he said, explaining that the mechanical workings were housed in a cylinder in the center of the merry-go-round. It looked like a dangerous place to play. An open door allowed visitors to peer inside and from his place in line Mike could see the naughty children playing in there.

The boy appeared to be about ten and the girl around eight. Mike was struck by their odd clothing. "I thought they were foreign," he said. "Their clothes looked like they were from the 1920s. The boy wore knickers and the girl wore a dress."

It did not occur to Mike that the two were ethereal beings. Over fifteen years passed and he did not give the encounter much thought until he began exploring a favorite hobby—*ghost hunting*. He set up a Web site devoted to haunted places in Portland. And then one day, he opened an e-mail that sent a chill skipping down his spine.

". . . I was wondering if you've ever heard of any sightings at the carousel up at Jantzen Beach," wrote Sarah Robinson. She explained that she had been researching, trying to learn if there had ever been an accident on the carousel, as she had seen the ghosts of two children playing on it.

". . .When I was a small child, I saw two children, a boy and a girl, play-ing in the center of it through an open door . . ." She went on to say that they were dressed in 1920s attire and she had seen them several times—but only when the door to the machinery was open.

"It wasn't until I got that letter from Sarah that I *knew*," Mike Ball told me. He cast his memory back and tried to recall details as I grilled him. After so many years, he could not remember the color of the chil-dren's hair or exactly what he'd heard them say. He remembered that they whispered to each other. "Every once in a while, they'd stop and gaze off to the right, as if they were looking for someone," said Mike.

I asked him if his daughters had seen the mysterious children too. "I don't think they did," he said. His girls are grown now, the youngest twenty-two. "They've seen my Web site and know the story but they don't remember seeing the children," he said.

While Mike's children are now adults, two others will never grow up. According to Sarah, the little ghosts were recently seen by her young son. *". . .When I moved back to North Portland, my husband and I took my oldest boy on the carousel a few times,"* read her posting on Mike's Web site. *"He was about one and a half. He liked it when the doors were closed and screamed if they were open, so we stopped taking him there. I didn't tell my husband a thing until last week when I took my son, alone, on a ride. He just turned three and he talks a LOT. While we were waiting for the ride to begin, I noticed that we were directly in front of the open door. I got a shiver and my son looked up at me and said, 'There's kids under there, Mama.' I said I knew and he said very seriously with some fear in his eyes, 'I don't want to go under there . . .'"*

When I spoke with Sarah, she described the scenario she'd wit-nessed as a child in the exact way that Mike had. Unaware of Mike's description, she, too, remembered that the boy wore knickers.

"Mike said the boy wore knickers when he saw the children twenty years ago!" I told her.

"It's funny that he saw them twenty years ago," said Sarah. "That was around the last time I saw them—when I was eight. I saw them about three times—but only when the door to the machinery was open. The first time I saw them I was three or four and I didn't like it. When I was eight, they wanted me to join them. That's what I felt.

They would stare me down. I always picked the outside horse because I didn't like to be close to them."

Each time the carousel horse glided past the open door, Sarah glanced down and saw the solemn faces of the two odd children peering up at her. She first visited the carousel with her mother and her little brother. When she tried to tell her mother about what she saw, her mother said, "You're pipe-dreaming."

The forlorn spirits of two children have been spotted on the historical Jantzen Beach carousel. Only those with a keen sixth sense seem to be able to see them. (Leslie Rule)

But Sarah knew she wasn't dreaming. The children were as real and solid-looking as everyone else at the mall that day but there was something about them that was creepy. She somehow sensed they were not of this world.

"The girl had long brown hair and she may have been wearing a big white bow," she said, as she tried to recall details from the long-ago sighting. "I think the boy was wearing suspenders and a white shirt and a flat hat. They were always huddled together and turned away from me when I first saw them. And then they would look at me."

When her young son, Benjamin, said he saw the children, Sarah looked for them. "I could feel them, but I couldn't see them," she said. She remembers the exact day—February 28, 2001. "It was the last free thing Benjamin would get to do because he was turning three the next day," she said. "He was really upset when we got home and wanted to talk about the kids. He felt really sad for them."

Sarah questioned him carefully to see if he would describe the same thing she had seen years before. "How many children did you see?" she asked him.

"Two."

"Two boys?"

"No," said Benjamin. "A boy and a girl. They wanted me to play with them."

"Did they say anything to you?" asked Sarah.

His little voice quivered as he said sadly, "They got hurt and they can't leave. They're stuck in there. The girl said, 'Don't throw him!'"

I asked Sarah what it was that had bothered her and Benjamin so much about the sighting. "What did you feel that is so upsetting?"

"Maybe it's the loneliness," she answered carefully, pointing out that she felt the two little souls are very alone. "It is a heavy, *heavy*, feeling—a trapped feeling."

Who are the ghosts who haunt the old carousel?

It has an interesting history. Built in 1921 at the C. W. Parker Amusement Company in Leavenworth, Kansas, at least one historian insists that the exquisite machine operated at the Venice Beach, California, Pier from 1921 to 1924. If indeed the carousel was there, my research indicates it would have operated adjacent to the roller coaster there. Interestingly, old newspaper articles report numerous fatalities on the coaster, some which occurred while the carousel was there. Most of the people killed during this time appear to have been teenage boys who stood up during the ride and were thrown to their deaths.

Thrown. That is the word that articles usually use to describe what happens to victims when they are catapulted from a coaster car. It brings to mind the thing that Benjamin heard the ghost child say. *"Don't throw him!"*

Is there a connection between the people killed on the coaster and the ghosts of the Jantzen Beach carousel? Possibly. I do not have all the history of the accidents on the Venice Beach Pier. Confused souls who died there could very likely have attached themselves to the merry-go-round.

Or is it possible that the two children were thrown from the roller coaster on the pier? Could they have been drowned by a suicidal parent who joined them in the ocean? Was the girl speaking to her mother or father when she said, "Don't throw him!"

One report says that the carousel was in a major fire there in 1924. The notorious 1924 fire, however, did not occur on the Venice Pier, but on the Ocean Park Pier, less than a mile away.

Was anyone harmed in the fire? Perhaps a boy and a girl?

After the fire, the merry-go-round spent several years in storage before it was moved to the Jantzen Beach Amusement Park in Portland in 1928. The 123-acre park was a focal point of fun for folks from miles around. With ballrooms and swimming pools and a funhouse and rides, the park entertained the crowds until 1970, when it was shut down and razed to make way for the Jantzen Beach Mall.

A death on the Big Dipper Roller Coaster reportedly contributed to the demise of the park. The carousel was set up in the mall, where it operated until 1995, when it underwent a half-million-dollar renovation. It is now the pride and joy of the new Jantzen Beach SuperCenter. Some visit for a nostalgic ride on a painted pony of the past, while others scrutinize it for a glimpse of a pair of strange children from another time.

At least one operator of the carousel is unhappy with the idea of ghosts there. When Mike posted Sarah's story on his Web site, he got an e-mail from an angry woman who said that the reports were nonsense and that she is annoyed when visitors ask her about the ghosts.

"She said she's worked there for years and has never seen any-thing," said Mike, who did not bother to respond to her—*or* to tell her that he himself had witnessed two very unusual children playing on the merry-go-round. Somehow, he didn't think she'd be convinced.

When it comes to ghost sightings, we can only speculate on why some people see them and others don't. Children and sensitive adults tend to see ghosts more than others. A leading theory is that these per-ceptive people have an ability to see into "the other side" in the same way that a musically talented person can identify a note or an artist can draw an accurate sketch.

As so few people can actually see the ghosts on the Parker carousel, it must indeed feel very lonely for the little stuck spirits, as Sarah Robinson sensed. It is no wonder that they ask those who *can* see them to come and play!

Amusement Vortex

The idea of ghosts clinging to amusement rides is fascinating. Why are so many vintage park rides haunted?

It is a question worth contemplating. It could be the combination of three things. First, a traumatic death may have occurred in or near the ride, causing confusion in a spirit that is so shocked by its sudden demise he or she may not realize it is dead. Second, the intense excite-ment focused on the ride by the living may create an energy that these confounded souls are drawn to.

And third, this writer theorizes on the possibility that the circular motion and unwavering pattern of the ride may create a kind of energy vortex. Like a whirlpool that draws surrounding objects into it, the rotating current is undetectable to humans yet irresistible to ghosts. They get caught in the predictable path of the ride, which may pres-ent itself as a force they cannot break through.

Cedar Point Ghost

Opened in 1870 on Lake Erie, in Sandusky, Ohio, Cedar Point is the second-oldest amusement park in America. The seasonal 364-acre park also boasts the biggest collection of rides and roller coasters in the world, and was once the site of a legendary haunted carousel. The 1921 Dentzel Carousel traveled from park to park and was moved to Cedar Point in 1971, where it stayed for over two decades. It was there that employees whispered about the ghostly lady who rode it at night.

Artist Shelley Gorny Schoenherr was unaware of the ghost stories when she visited Cedar Point. She was simply fascinated with historic carousels—so fascinated that she made them her favorite subject. Her life-sized renderings in pastels and oils depict carved animals from famous carousels. Yet as drawn as she is to the marvelous menageries, she cannot explain why one "plain old brownish horse" captivated her two decades ago.

"I spent several days in a row, one summer, going back and photographing it," confided the Detroit resident. She had no idea that the one horse that she was so inexplicably mesmerized by was haunted.

This antique postcard depicts the Midway at Cedar Point where the ghost of a woman in white has been seen at night. She resembles the lady in the forefront. (Author's Collection)

"I'd like to say it haunted me," said Shelley with a smile, "but the carving and the stature of the animal simply captivated me. Is this an example of the strange power it has over people? Without knowing a thing about the horse's history, I chose it above all the other magical animals on that carousel. Or did it choose *me*?"

During its time at Cedar Point, the Dentzel Carousel charmed children during the day and frightened employees at night. For it was then, when the lights were turning off and workers were sweeping up, that a ghost mounted the carousel horse. Witnesses swore that the carousel glowed as the specter rode around.

The ghost always chose the same horse that Shelley had. It was carved in 1924 by Carl Muller. Witnesses said the ghost was a woman in a long white dress.

The identity of the ethereal lady remains a mystery, though some speculate she may be the wife of the carver.

The carousel was eventually moved to Dorney Park. The haunted horse has a place of honor in the carousel museum at Cedar Point. Is it still haunted?

If anyone has seen the ghost of a woman in white in the carousel museum, perhaps they will write and let me know!

CEDAR POINT
1 CEDAR POINT DRIVE
SANDUSKY, OH 44870
(419) 627-2350

Eat, Drink, and Be Scary!

Many theorize that ghosts are drawn in death to the same things they were drawn to in life. If this is true, that would certainly explain the proliferation of haunted restaurants and bars. In the places that people gather to eat, drink, and be merry, so do spirits. The following are just a few examples:

Ghostly Exposure

"Roslyn is the most haunted place I know of," Steve Ojurovich, owner of the Pioneer Restaurant and Sody-licious Bar, said of the town he calls home. Nestled in the Cascade Mountains in central Washington, Roslyn was established by the Northern Pacific Railroad in 1886 as a coal mining town. Made famous when used as the setting for the mythical town of Cicely, Alaska, in the quirky hit television program *Northern Exposure*, which debuted in 1990, Roslyn is still recognizable to fans of the show who visit the small rustic town for the nostalgia, as well as for snowmobile and horse riding.

While known for its TV exposure, Roslyn is not yet well known for its *ghostly* exposure. Residents say the place is crawling with ghosts. In fact, Steve claims six of the town's ghosts inhabit his restaurant and bar. "I saw the first one the night I bought the place four years ago," he confided. He was in the downstairs bar area, cleaning up, when he saw a figure from the corner of his eye. "I thought it was my dad, so I called to him." When there was no reply, he went in search of him but the place was empty and the doors locked. He'd no sooner gone back to his chores when he saw him again. "He looked like a logger, with a blue plaid shirt and jeans on. And he had a beard."

Since then, the bearded ghost has been seen frequently, sometimes walking in the hallway by the bathrooms and sometimes walking past the cooler. He is always accompanied by the strong scent of cigarette smoke.

Who is he?

According to Steve, he just might be the fellow his grandpa once told him about—the fellow who "poked his nose where it didn't belong."

Steve, a fourth-generation Roslyn resident, is a walking history book of the town's past. His great-grandfather came from Croatia to mine coal in Roslyn and the family has been here ever since. The building that houses his restaurant and bar was once the Pioneer Grocery Store. Before that it was a Sears and Roebuck that went out of business when it couldn't compete with the other local merchants, he explained. The basement was once a Sody-licious soda bottling company where during prohibition more potent drinks were surreptitiously brewed. Secret underground tunnels hid

Steve Ojurovich, owner of the Pioneer Restaurant and Sody-licious Bar, often encounters ghosts there. (Leslie Rule)

the illegal activity and it was there that a visiting stranger decided to snoop around. "According to my grandpa, the man was shot and killed right there," said Steve, pointing to the cooler behind the bar, where the entrance to the tunnel was long ago sealed up. "And that's where we see the ghost."

I had brought my electromagnetic field detector along on this trip and I lifted the popular handheld ghost-hunting device and pointed it to where Steve gestured. It instantly measured high on the scale, indicating energy where there was no logical explanation for the source.

"And we see him over here," said Steve, pointing to the hallway that runs past the small restrooms. Once again, the EMFD registered high on the scale as I pointed it in the areas where the specter was said to walk.

Upstairs in the two-story restaurant, a woman's ghost was once seen peering from the window. It was late and Steve and the bartender had just closed up and were shooting the breeze on the sidewalk when they saw her. She stood in the restaurant window, gazing out at the street. "She wore a white blouse with puffy sleeves," said Steve. "Her hair was parted in the middle, braided, and pulled back from her face."

Steve's mother, Marianne Ojurovich, thinks she knows who the ghost is. The description matches that of the woman who owned the grocery store where Marianne's family shopped for many years. Steve was too young to have known Edna, but when he described her to his mother, she nodded her head as she remembered. Edna died decades ago of natural causes in her senior years, but the apparition appeared as she had looked in younger days. "I can't say for certain it was Edna," said Marianne, "but I think it was her. She always wore her hair like that."

Edna's apartment had once occupied the space that serves as the Pioneer Restaurant kitchen and Steve often senses her presence there. "She walked through me once," Steve said. "It was the most exhilarating experience I ever had."

He was in the kitchen, he said, when he sensed the ghost move through him. "I felt tingling all the way to my fingertips and toes."

Steve believes that another woman's ghost shares the downstairs bar with the logger. "She doesn't know she's dead," he said, relying on his natural strong sixth sense to come to that conclusion. "The ghosts here have bothered me only once," he added, and described an incident that left him uneasy. "Against my wishes, one of my employees had used a

Ouija board here. I was at the cash register when a dark shadow shot up over my head and went across the room."

Sometimes the ghosts make mischief at the Pioneer Restaurant. Marianne recalls the time that a young woman was so shocked that she never returned after a bottle of wine suddenly exited the wine rack, shot through the air, and shattered beside her. "The bottle had not been opened," Marianne said. "I could see it was unopened because I picked up the broken glass myself. There was no way that gasses could have been built up to cause the bottle to explode."

Another time, Marianne's husband, Joe, was sitting quietly in the same area when a bottle of gin lifted up off the bar and dropped at his feet. "He doesn't believe in ghosts," said Marianne, who smiled when she remembered how unsettled he was by the unexplained occurrence. "He doesn't like to talk about it."

Hide and Seek

Next door to the Pioneer Restaurant is the Brick Tavern, the tavern used as a favorite setting for *Northern Exposure*. Fans might gaze around the familiar rustic watering hole and expect to see the characters Holling and Shelly serving beer behind the bar. While the actors have moved on, *others* have left something behind. Quite possibly, their souls.

Bartender Jeremy Kaynor still seemed shaken as he set down a tray and told me about the encounter he had when he began working at the Brick Tavern in the summer of 2003. He and a roommate shared an upstairs apartment and one night, shortly after moving in, they glanced at the security monitor, which kept them tuned in to the scene at the bar.

The bar was closed and buttoned up tight for the night, but movement on the monitor caught their attention. "There was a little girl staring at us!" said Jeremy. He pointed out the tiny white camera in the corner of the ceiling. "See that camera?" he asked me.

After scrutinizing the ceiling for a moment, I noticed it and nodded.

"She was just standing there, staring up at the camera," said Jeremy. She was little—about as tall as the pool tables. Her blouse was white with puffy sleeves."

When you drink at the Brick Tavern in Roslyn, Washington, the ghosts of miners might join you. (Leslie Rule)

When his roommate got up and started running to go check out the scene, Jeremy watched the monitor and saw the little girl run at the same time—as if *she* could see them through the camera too. "She ran behind the pool tables," said Jeremy. The guys searched, but there was no sign of anyone there.

When a coworker later learned that Jeremy had seen a ghost, she casually asked him, "Oh, did you see the man or the little girl?"

That was it for Jeremy. He gave notice to move out of his apartment. "I'll work here, but I'm not going to live here," he said, and related another incident when owner, Wanda Najar, heard the sound of someone chopping wood in the bar in the middle of the night. Again, the Brick Tavern was closed and the doors were barred from the inside.

"Jeremy, are you making that noise?" Wanda called to him. "Are you chopping wood?"

He answered in the negative and together they went downstairs and found that a chair in the bar had been chopped into pieces.

This brings to mind the logger's ghost, who has been seen frequently next door at Steve's Sody-licious Bar. A logger, of course, would be adept with an ax.

Does the bearded specter wander between the two places?

Or perhaps it was the ghost of one of the miners who once populated the town. They, too, used axes in their work.

While Roslyn's bars don't allow *minors*, they couldn't stop *miners* from frequenting their establishments even if they wanted to, for the ghosts of these dead men are persistent. Steve mentioned a house in town where his friends looked into a hole beneath it and saw something unexpected. "They saw the faces of the miners," he told me.

Today Roslyn's population is around a thousand people, far less than at its peak in 1910, when four thousand folks lived there. Over twenty different ethnic groups lived together as the men in the families worked the coal mines. In its heyday, nearly two million tons of coal a year were produced. It was an honest living but it was hard, dirty, and sometimes dangerous work. Accidents happened and miners were sometimes killed.

According to Marianne Ojurovich, the carbide lights on the miners' hats produced acetylene gas, which at times built up and created deadly explosions.

When the steam locomotives were replaced with diesels in the 1920s, the mines gradually began to shut down. Logging became the major occupation there for a while.

Loggers or miners or merchants, they've all bellied up to the bar at the Brick Tavern, which is the oldest licensed bar in the state of Washington. It opened its doors in 1889 and has seen some rowdy characters come and go. Worn wooden floors, high brick walls, and a spittoon that runs like a little river beside the bar all add to the rustic ambience.

In addition to the apparitions seen there, witnesses have also heard phantom piano music. Staff have left shots of whiskey out on the bar at night, hoping to appease the rambunctious spirits, only to find the glasses empty the next day.

Downstairs, the remnants of an old jail cell recall a time when miners-turned-criminals were locked up there. Curiously, a tombstone for a man named William Thomas sits in one of the old cells. Is he buried there? If so, is his ghost one of the restless ones who roam Roslyn?

Many of the mysteries of the historic town are buried and may remain that way forever.

Ghost Makers

Much of the paranormal activity in Roslyn, Washington, is credited to the ghosts of miners who were tragically killed there at work. The worst explosion killed forty-five men in May 1892. The Cusworth family was one that lost two members. Joseph was forty-four and his son Joe was not yet twenty.

An October 1909 explosion killed sixteen men in mine number four, at 1 P.M. on a Sunday. While the families of those killed were grieving the tragic loss, others were counting their blessings because just the day before, a Saturday, five hundred men were down in the same mines and would certainly have perished if the explosion had occurred twenty-four hours earlier.

Excerpt from the *Ellensburg Dawn*, October 7, 1909, edition:

. . . Without warning of any kind, the terrific explosion shook the town and broke windows half a mile away from the shaft. A sheet of flames shot out of the shaft 150 feet in the air for several minutes. There were two distinct explosions following close after each other like rapid gun firing. The tiple [sic] over the shaft and the other outbuildings instantly broke into flames before anyone got near. The dead are:

James E. Jones, pumpman, aged 21, single.
Ben Hardy, tracklayer, aged 60, married.

Dominick Bartolera, helper, aged 45, married.
Philip Pozarich, laborer, aged 45, married.
Aaron Isaacson, tracklayer, aged 30, married.
Carl Berger, foreman, aged 36, married.
Tom Marsolich, laborer, aged 30, married.
Geo. Tomich, laborer, aged 28, married.
Otis Newhouse, outside superintendent, aged 40 married.
James Gurrell, trackman, aged 50, married.
William Arundale, trackman, aged 40, married.

Excerpt from the *Cle Elum Echo,* October 9, 1909, edition:
. . . Men known to have been down in the mine and who probably will
never be found, as the intense heat must have cremated them:
Daniel Hardy, Company Man; married.
Dom Bartolero, company man; leaves a family.
J. E. Jones, assistant company man; single, son of hoising engineer.
Tom Marsolyn, company man; single.
Philip Pozarich, company man; single.

The leading theory among parapsychologists is that traumatic, sudden death is most commonly tied to a haunted place. The mine disasters in Roslyn certainly qualify as ghost makers.

I Hear You Knocking

When I dined at Albuquerque's famous haunted Luna Mansion, I hoped to see a ghost. Of course, I *always* hope to see a ghost while researching—though I wonder whether my readers would believe me if I ever *did* actually see one.

I worry that they will cluck their tongues and shake their heads. *How convenient that she just happened to see a ghost while looking for one!* Still, I had my eyes peeled when I arrived right before dusk and circled the outside of the impressive columned mansion. I photographed it from every angle and as I stood on the grass and stared at the back of the house, I tried to will the spirit of Josefita Otero to appear.

No such luck.

The big yard was eerily quiet with not a soul in sight. Everyone was inside eating. I soon joined my friend, fellow writer Cheri Eicher, at a window table in the elegant dining room, where paintings of the family who had once lived there adorned the walls.

As we ate, we queried our waiter, who told us that he had once seen the mansion's ghost. "It was Josefita," he told us. "She was on the staircase."

With permission to enter the kitchen, I found several chefs busily chopping and stirring. "Have any of you ever seen the ghost?" I asked, after explaining that I was writing a book.

"No," one of the chefs replied. "But something strange just happened. Someone knocked on the door." He pointed to the kitchen's backdoor. "When we opened it, no one was there. It happened twice in the last half hour!"

At first I thought they were pulling my leg, but they were all insistent that they had indeed heard knocking and that before tonight this had never occurred.

How odd, I thought, that this should happen around the time that I had been circling the building. Was the Luna Mansion ghost aware of my quest? Was this her way of accommodating me?

Diners at the Luna Mansion choose this spot for the fine food as well as for a chance to glimpse a ghost. (Leslie Rule)

It seems that she wants her existence known. A waitress who was bustling by with a pitcher of water stopped to tell me about the night a couple asked her about the ghost. "I told them I didn't believe the stories about the ghosts," she said. "And then when I started to walk away, something strange happened to the man at the next table. His plate flipped."

Everyone had stopped eating and stared at the plate full of fine cuisine, now inexplicably turned upside down in front of the bewildered diner.

Had the resident ghost flipped the plate?

It wasn't the type of behavior expected of Josefita. Josefita Manderfield Otero (affectionately known as Pepe) once lived in the home. A talented gardener and painter, she was a creative and kind soul. She was not the type to flip someone's dinner.

Perhaps her spirit simply did not want to be dismissed. The mess was whisked away and a new meal was brought to the diner. The waitress never again doubted the ghost's existence.

This painting of Josefita Otero hangs on a wall inside the Luna Mansion, where her friendly ghost is seen. (Leslie Rule)

The staff at Luna Mansion told us about the time when a manager's young child was upstairs alone. Later she told her father that "a nice lady read me a story . . ."

When the child spotted a painting of Josefita, she exclaimed, "That's *her*! That's the lady who read to me!"

If you have any doubts about ghosts, consider a visit to the Luna Mansion restaurant. At the very least you will have a wonderful meal. And if you are *really* lucky, you may catch a glimpse of Josefita.

Hungry Ghosts

They hate to eat and run, but sometimes customers *do* leave running when they encounter something that isn't on the menu in the following restaurants and bars:

Where's the Fire?

This charming eatery is adorned with firehouse relics and named for the playful moniker of the steam pumpers and engines that served firemen in the late 1800s. It is, in fact, located inside Erie's Fire House No. 1. The 1907 building has definitely seen its share of drama. In 1915, the city's first firefighter, John J. Donavan, lost his life in the line of duty. He died while pulling Chief McMahon to safety during a surging flood. The chief died less than three weeks later from overexposure. Sadly, they were not the last to succumb to the dangers of the job, for many brave people died over the years. Their spirits may reside there, but it is the ghost of a little boy who materializes in the restaurant.

Though owners Bruce and Mary Ellen Hemme have not seen him, both customers and employees have. "A waitress once saw the ghost run through a cook," said Mary Ellen, describing

The Pufferbelly Restaurant is housed in the old fire station. A stubborn little ghost refuses to leave. (Leslie Rule)

how the cook couldn't see the ghost but he suddenly shuddered and said, "Oh God, I just got the biggest chill!"

The ghost is believed to belong to a paperboy who collected his newspapers at the fire station in the 1960s. The child had a dangerous habit of jumping on the back of the newspaper delivery truck. One day, he fell off and the truck backed over him.

Retired firemen who lunch at Pufferbelly's remember the child. One asked knowingly, "Have you seen the ghost of a boy here?"

Mary Ellen has heard the sound of little feet running when she is alone in the building. "I hear lots of odd noises," she said. "Sometimes I hear a pop gun being used when no one is here."

THE PUFFERBELLY RESTAURANT
414 FRENCH STREET
ERIE, PA 16507
(814) 454-1557
WWW.THEPUFFERBELLY.COM

Check, Please!

Casa de Pasta's owner and chef, Dominick Dardano, does not believe in ghosts. He laughs at reports that ghosts share Canandaigua's favorite Italian haunt—a critically acclaimed restaurant in a historic brick house. Yet several waitresses insist that while diners enjoy the fine cuisine, one hungry-looking little girl never gets to chow down. The ghostly child appears to be about six with long blonde hair that flows past her shoulders. She's been seen sitting quietly at a table. When a waitress approached, she vanished. Servers also report that candles inexplicably ignite themselves.

CASA DE PASTA
125 BEMIS STREET
CANANDAIGUA, NY 14424
(585) 394-3710
WWW.CASA-DE-PASTA.COM

One hungry guest at Casa de Pasta, a popular Canandaigua restaurant, never gets to eat. (Leslie Rule)

Spirits of the Dead

Be silent in that solitude,
Which is not loneliness—for then
The spirits of the dead, who stood
In life before thee, are again
In death around thee, and their will
Shall overshadow thee: be still.

Excerpt from "Spirits of the Dead," 1827, by Edgar Allan Poe

Fells Point, a historic waterfront section of Baltimore, Maryland, is home to The Horse You Came in On. This popular pub is purported to have been one of Edgar Allan Poe's favorite drinking places.

Some insist that it is the famous poet's restless spirit who haunts the bar. Paranormal activity includes a swinging chandelier and a cash register drawer that mysteriously opens by itself.

THE HORSE YOU CAME IN ON
1626 THAMES STREET
FELLS POINT
BALTIMORE, MD 21231
(410) 327-8111

Under the Table

Speaking of horsey taverns and ghostly poets, the White Horse Tavern in New York is said to be haunted by Dylan Thomas. It is there that the poet is said to have collapsed and died after guzzling numerous shots of scotch in 1953.

Reportedly, his last words were, "I just had my sixteenth whiskey."

Witnesses report that Dylan Thomas's ghost still likes to rotate his favorite corner table—an odd habit he had in life.

WHITE HORSE TAVERN
567 HUDSON STREET AT WEST ELEVENTH STREET
NEW YORK, NY 10014
(212) 243-9260

After You, Madam

Don't expect to buy shoes for your horse in Lafitte's Blacksmith Shop in New Orleans, for it is not *really* a blacksmith shop, but a popular bar. Housed in a French Quarter historic structure, it is believed to be home to the ghost of Jean Lafitte, "the gentleman pirate." Legend has it that Lafitte used the building as a front, operating a blacksmith shop there to cover shadier activities.

Today the candlelit bar with the flickering fireplace is a favorite haunt for jazz enthusiasts who visit for the music as well as the rustic ambience.

Built before 1772, the French-styled building survived the two terrifying fires of the late eighteenth century. In 1788 and 1794 infernos destroyed hundreds of buildings. Then under Spanish domain, the area was rebuilt with Spanish influence apparent in the architecture. Lafitte's Blacksmith Shop is one of the rare leftover original "French architecture" structures in the area. Perhaps it is this distinction that draws spirits inside. Customers report encountering a number of apparitions here. Some say the pirate's ghost guards the fireplace, where his treasure may be hidden.

LAFITTE'S BLACKSMITH SHOP
941 BOURBON STREET
NEW ORLEANS, LA 70116
(504) 523-0066

Is This Seat Taken?

You're never drinking alone at Amy's Ritz in Chippewa Falls, Wisconsin. The seat beside you may look empty, but you just might have some company. Folks say they feel a presence at the tavern that could explain why objects are sometimes inexplicably moved around. Some of the bartenders refuse to venture into the basement, but owner Amy Anderson is not afraid, though she and her father, John Anderson, have both seen the ghost of a short man there who is sometimes accompanied by a rush of icy air.

AMY'S RITZ
114 WEST RIVER STREET
CHIPPEWA FALLS, WI 54729
(715) 726-8710

Scarlett O'*Scara's*

"Splish, splash, I was taking a bath . . ."

It's the upbeat beginning to a popular old song.

"And then I drowned but I'm still around" would be the next line if the singer was the legendary ghost of Scarlett O'Hara's haunted bar! For he is—*indeed*—still around!

Scarlett O'Hara's, in an old building in downtown St. Augustine, is known for its fine food and live entertainment. The upstairs bar is said to be the domain of a man who long ago drowned in a bathtub there. Witnesses insist that the wee hours of the morning bring with them the inexplicable sound of splashing and eerie moaning.

SCARLETT O'HARA'S BAR AND RESTAURANT

70 HYPOLITA STREET

ST. AUGUSTINE, FL 32084

(904) 824-6535

WWW.SCARLETTOHARAS.NET

Table for Two

Two ghosts are seen at this Capitol Hill, Seattle, bar. Both appear to be from the 1930s. An elegant lady in an evening gown appears on the balcony level, where she has been spotted watching the piano player. Others have seen the ghost of a man in a dark suit and a fedora. The man seems to be searching for someone—perhaps the beautiful phantom.

BALTIC ROOM

1207 PINE STREET

SEATTLE, WA 98101

(206) 625-4444

Someone's in the Kitchen

A charming historic house in Sumner, Washington, has been turned into the Sleighbells Christmas Shoppe & Café, where customers can enjoy lunch or shop for exquisite Christmas ornaments year-round. Employees here have encountered the spirit of Lola, an old woman

The spirit of a friendly old woman lives at the Sleighbells Christmas Shoppe & Café in Sumner, Washington. (Leslie Rule)

who once owned the house. She has been seen in the kitchen as well as in other parts of the house. Often it is just her silhouette that is seen. She is said to be a friendly presence.

SLEIGHBELLS CHRISTMAS SHOPPE & CAFÉ
1711 ELM STREET
SUMNER, WA 98390
(253) 826-5501

A mischievous spirit sometimes tugs on customers' hair at the Inn Philadelphia. (Leslie Rule)

Make Mine a Double

The Inn Philadelphia is a cozy restaurant recommended to those who savor fine cuisine in a romantic setting. Co-owner George Lutz is happy to share ghost stories with curious diners. Housed in a historic brick duplex on a narrow Philadelphia street, the one-time residence draws people with its artfully prepared food, street-level piano bar, and reputation as a haunted spot. "I think that one of the ghosts is a little girl," admitted George, adding that she may have died in a fire there many years ago.

When he and business partner Phil Orchowski opened the restaurant in 1993, they immediately sensed they had a very special place on their hands. Phenomena at the Inn Philadelphia include the inexplicable sound of doors opening and closing, a spinning chandelier in the ballroom, and the occasional materialization of apparitions. An unseen presence sometimes pinches guests or tugs on their hair.

Lutz was once enjoying conversation with customers at the bar when the group turned white with shock. They all started talking and pointing at once and he turned around to see nothing amiss. They explained that a ghost had emerged from the closet behind him and vanished into the wall.

INN PHILADELPHIA
251–253 SOUTH CAMAC STREET
PHILADELPHIA, PA 19107
(215) 732-8630

Ghosts in the News

The McScary Meal

REPORTER BUCK WOLF OF ABC NEWS joked that when customers eat at the McDonald's in Lewiston, New York, they "sometimes get a shake, even if they order a Coke."

In his October 2002 "Wolf Report," he said that the fast-food restaurant was haunted. According to the account, the ghost of William Morgan, who died in 1826 under suspicious circumstances, has been seen by the restaurant manager. Workers there describe seeing the milk-white apparition of an old man. They have also heard strange voices. One maintenance man was so frightened that he quit after a ghostly encounter.

Located in Lewiston's Frontier House, the McDonald's has long been known as a haunted spot. While sightings escalated in the 1970s, they are reportedly less frequent now.

MCDONALD'S
460 CENTER STREET
LEWISTON, NY 14092
(716) 754-9458

Four-Footed Spirits

Wendy Yaddock and I have been friends since we were five years old. Over the years we sometimes drift apart and too much time might go by between talks. But we always send each other birthday cards and no matter what is happening in our lives, we always have one thing in common. *Cats.* We love them.

Wendy knew that she could share something with me that I would understand. When Goofer, her beloved cat, passed away, she was devastated. He was one of those special, once-in-a-lifetime cats. When he looked at Wendy and she looked at him, they had a connection that did not need words. He was always there to comfort her when she was feeling sad. With Goofer gone, she felt a painful void. "I tried to work through my grief in the next few weeks and thought of him often," said Wendy. "One day I was on my couch when I saw him. He was walking through the room, holding his tail up high."

She stared in amazement at the slightly transparent cat before he vanished. Since then, Wendy has seen him three times and her son has spotted him once. "I miss my cat," she told me. "But I feel comforted in knowing that we are really still together."

While Wendy's story is heartwarming, it is not unique. Our animals love us and they often stick around after death takes their physical bodies.

The following stories tell of animals whose spirits have lived beyond their bodies:

The White Dog

When Kathleen Lee is asked about the scariest incident of her life, she casts her memory back to the 1960s when she was a cute twelve-year-old girl with fire-red hair that fell to her waist.

The Ontario mother of six remembers how her own mother struggled to raise five kids alone. The year she started junior high school, Kathleen, her sister, and her three brothers moved with their mother to a drafty farmhouse in the middle of six acres of land in Whonnock, British Columbia. "It was a rental house," said Kathleen. "It once belonged to a Japanese family and they lost it when they were sent to an internment camp during the war."

The kids found old faded Japanese newspapers in the attic. Kathleen felt sad for the family she knew had once loved the home. The long driveway that led to the secluded two-story house was lined with Japanese cherry and plum trees and the overgrown land still harbored beautiful oriental shrubbery, long ago planted by loving hands.

Sometimes Kathleen and her siblings were a little spooked on the isolated property, especially when the kids at school whispered about the nearby institute for the criminally insane. "It scared us," she admitted. "We worried someone would escape."

One dreary February afternoon the family was surprised to find a visitor at their door. "It was a beautiful white dog," said Kathleen. "He was *so* beautiful that even my mother was impressed and she is not a dog person."

The husky-like dog had a thick fluffy coat. Her fur was pure white. Oddly so. Most white dogs, Kathleen points out, have a little yellow or beige tones mixed into their fur. But the Carnegies' visitor had startling, snow white fur.

The dog watched the children with inquisitive, friendly eyes. "My brother tried to touch her, but she backed away," said Kathleen. The curious canine seemed to want to join the family, yet she shied away when anyone came near.

The Carnegie kids put food and water out for the dog, hoping their mother would let them keep her. She had a collar with a tag hanging from it, but they could never get close enough to her to read it. Meanwhile, their dog, Scampy, a medium-sized mixed breed, stayed in the backyard. This was a little peculiar, as Scampy normally raced around the house, his tail wagging, eager to greet visitors—dogs and people alike.

That night Kathleen watched television until she fell asleep on the living room sofa. It was 2 A.M. when she woke with a start to an odd mixture of noises. The static of the TV was drowned out by the keening howl of Scampy. Kathleen sat up quickly. "I thought something was wrong with Scampy," she said. Then she realized that the white dog, still on the front porch, was also making noise—a low, throaty growl.

Puzzled, Kathleen got up. The moon was full and filled the room with a cold white light. Kathleen glanced at the front door and froze. There, silhouetted against the door's window, was a tall figure.

The bright moonlight behind him blotted out his features. For a second, she wondered if she were looking at her own shadow. "I moved my head, but he didn't move," she said. Cold terror filled her belly and her feet seemed stuck to the floor. "I could see the outline of his shoulders, neck, and jaw, but he was so big that he was taller than the door. I could not see the top of his head.

"I knew he could see me. I was so frightened it seemed like my heart stopped. I could not even scream. I just couldn't believe that this was happening to me. We were locked there, with him watching me. He was menacing. I knew whatever was on his mind couldn't be good."

Suddenly the white dog's growl turned into a ferocious roar. Kathleen could not see the dog, yet she knew the animal lunged at the intruder. "I saw the man's head move from the window."

Kathleen ran to her mother's room and watched from the window as the white dog chased the stranger up the long driveway. "It was too dark to see the man." Only the dog was visible, glowing white in the moonlight as she raced away.

"I went looking for the dog the next morning," said Kathleen. But the animal had vanished as quickly as it had appeared. She stood on the porch, wondering what had become of the mysterious creature. Then her eyes fell on the dishes they had set out for the dog. "They were still filled to the brim," said Kathleen. "The food and water had not been touched."

"I showed my mother," Kathleen remembered. "When she saw the food hadn't been touched, she said, 'That dog was sent by God to protect us.'"

The dog, they decided, had to be either an angel or a ghost. They checked with all the neighbors and no one else had seen or heard of the pure white dog.

"Scampy refused to come around to the front of the house for several days," said Kathleen. "My brother Gary tried to drag him, but he wouldn't budge."

Was the white dog an ethereal being? The fact that she did not touch food or water for the twelve hours she had sat on the porch was strange. And why did no one in the community know anything about such an unusual-looking dog? Wouldn't someone else have noticed the animal?

Scampy's behavior, too, pointed to the possibility that the white dog may have been from another plane. Why wouldn't the friendly Scampy interact with the dog?

The menacing intruder was another puzzling element. Was it possible, that he, too, was a ghost? Or was he a patient, escaped or discharged from the nearby criminally insane institution?

If his presence was ghostly, could it have anything to do with the Japanese family who was removed from their home? Was the white dog a ghost of a pet of the Japanese family who suffered the injustice of internment?

Perhaps she had come back to make sure another family would not lose anything precious.

Out to Pasture

Jessie Johnson was a sophomore in high school on the winter morning she trudged through the snow to the barn to prepare breakfast for her four horses. It was 1994 and a heavy snow had fallen on the Ohio Valley, where the Johnson family lived on fifteen wooded acres.

As Jessie, her parents, and her eleven-year-old brother, Adam, filled pails with oats, the horses played in the snow in the pasture. It was a peaceful scene. The little farmhouse, the trees, and the long driveway that led to their home were all swaddled in white. Joey, their dark brown mare, pranced in the snow. She tossed her head, playful as a colt, as she danced about in the bright white world.

Suddenly, the sound of a gunshot shattered the peace.

The family was devastated to find Joey dying from a hunter's bullet. "I held her head," remembered Jessie. "It had snowed so much that the roads were too bad for the vet to get there in time to save her. It was horrible."

The careless hunter had thought he was shooting at a deer and discovered the distraught family when he arrived to collect his bounty.

It was the worst day of fifteen-year-old Jessie's life. The sweet-natured quarter horse with the white star on her forehead was a year older than she and had been born on the farm. Jessie had shown her in the 4-H Club. The gentle mare had always been part of her childhood.

"The horses were in our yard, right next to our house," Jessie stressed. "He shouldn't have been hunting there. It turned out he was a substitute teacher and he showed up at my school a few weeks later."

Jessie marched up to the teacher after class and spat, "You murdered my horse."

He shrugged and said, "I'm sorry."

"I don't care," she retorted, and stomped off. Though the Johnsons were awarded a cash settlement for Joey in a civil suit, and they purchased another horse, it did little to ease their grief. Joey had been part of their family. No amount of money—no other horse—could replace her.

The ground was frozen on that awful day Joey died. A kind neighbor showed up with his tractor and dug her grave beneath the tree where the mare had loved to graze. "It is at the end of our driveway. It was her favorite place. She was always standing there," remembered Jessie.

The seasons changed and the snow melted. Tiny wildflowers poked their heads up around the roots of Joey's tree. The Johnson family noticed something odd. When the horses were in the fenced-off area on the other side of the driveway, they would stand beside the fence and stick their heads over it, staring at the tree where Joey was buried.

There were four horses again. Joker, the newcomer, joined the others. Penny, Joey's mother, was such a bright red that she resembled a new penny shining in the sun. Nugget, Joey's son, was also bright red. Image, the pony, rounded out the foursome. The herd clustered together, staring over the fence at something beneath the tree—something no one else could see.

Springtime turned into summer and others began to see what the horses saw.

"My brother saw her first," said Jessie. Adam Johnson was sauntering up the hill to the end of the driveway on a summer morning when he passed the tree. "Hello, Joey," said the eleven-year-old as he saw the brown mare. He glanced away and then stopped in his tracks as realization flooded over him. *Joey was dead.*

When he looked back, the horse was gone. But he had seen her.

"He wasn't scared," said Jessie. "He was just a little unnerved."

A year later, it was summertime once again and Jessie was driving home after a night out with friends. "It was around 11 P.M., my curfew, as I pulled into the driveway," she confided. As she headed down the driveway, her headlights lit up the tree and there, grazing beneath it, was her beloved horse. "The other horses were all in the barn for the night," said Jessie. "I knew it was Joey."

She gazed at her for a full thirty seconds. The brown quarter horse appeared as solid and real as any living being. Then the animal dissolved before her eyes.

Tears burned Jessie's eyes as she sat in her car. "It brought back so many memories," she said.

Before long, every member of the Johnson family caught glimpses of the horse. "My father saw her too," said Jessie. "He doesn't believe in ghosts, but he saw her. He would tell us about it and then quickly change the subject."

Joey's spirit was spotted regularly. Jessie sometimes saw her when she looked out her bedroom window. "She was always under the tree," she said.

A few years after the tragic death of Joey, Penny died of natural causes. Her spirit, too, has been seen on the Johnson acreage. "Penny was my horse," said Jessie's mother, Cheryl Johnson. "I'd gotten her when I was sixteen. She was thirty-one when she died."

Penny, a registered quarter horse, was four years old when she came into Cheryl's life. Cheryl immediately fell in love with her. "She had a diamond star on her face, a white snip on her nose, and two white 'socks' halfway up her legs," said Cheryl. "When she died in 1997, we buried her where she liked to stand, under an ash tree."

A couple of months later it was dusk as Cheryl and her husband, Steve, were bringing the horses to the barn for the night. Cheryl was beside the barn with the horses gathered around her and Steve was on the road on the hill above. He called down to his wife, saying that one of the horses was grazing beneath the ash tree."

"It's not one of ours," Cheryl yelled to him. "I've got them all around me."

She looked up at the tree, and there in the dimming light, she saw the distinctive outline of a horse beneath it. "The image was there for a long time," she said. As she watched, it eventually dissolved into the shadows.

Jessie now lives in Anaheim, California, where she is a counselor who works with children. "The horses are still seen," she said. "It makes my mom happy. She's glad their spirits are still around."

The Smallest Ghost

Ghosts come in all sizes. While the animal spirits in the previous story might seem larger than life, others are just itsy-bitsy ghosts. Carlie Parrish was eleven years old when she fell in love with a tiny fluff of a creature she could cradle in her hand. Bubbles, the hamster, was just a baby when the Milton Keynes, England, girl began to nurture him. "He was a Christmas gift," she said.

She was devoted to her new friend. She couldn't help but smile when he looked up at her with his shiny dark eyes and wiggled his little nose. He lived in her room, in a little cage complete with an exercise wheel. "He was very active at night," said Carlie as she remembered one of her favorite childhood pets. Each night she fell asleep to the reassuring squeak of the exercise wheel as Bubbles scampered around. And around. *And around.* "At night he was constantly on that wheel," she said.

Bubbles died when he was two years old, and Carlie was inconsolable. "I screamed for hours," she confided.

"After he died, I didn't want the cage in my room, so my mum put it in the garage," Carlie said. But the fact that his cage was no longer in her room did not seem to deter the feisty little spirit of Bubbles. In the dark of her room, Carlie snuggled beneath the covers and was about to drift off to sleep when a sound startled her. It was the distinctive squeak of Bubbles's hamster wheel.

Then thirteen years old, Carlie was frightened by the sound. *Bubbles was gone and so was his cage. How could it be?*

Night after night, hour after hour, she lay in the dark and listened to the squeak of the exercise wheel. Spooked by the occurrence, she began to wear ear plugs to bed. "I also used to leave the hall light on at night. I never looked toward where the noise came from, because once I was in bed, I wouldn't move again until it was light. It really scared me."

After about six months, Carlie welcomed two new friends into her life. A pair of gerbils took up residence in her room and the phantom sounds of Bubbles abruptly stopped.

An adult now, Carlie is no longer frightened by the idea of a spirit pet sticking around. She still remembers Bubbles fondly. "I loved him to bits," she said.

Judging by the fact he stayed so long, it seems that Bubbles was attached to her too.

𝕲𝖍𝖔𝖘𝖙𝖘 𝖎𝖓 𝖙𝖍𝖊 𝕹𝖊𝖜𝖘

Move Over, Scooby-Doo!

WHILE MANY PEOPLE HAVE REPORTED sightings of ghostly animals, animals have also demonstrated that *they* can see ghosts. The *Raleigh (North Carolina) News & Observer* reported on a rottweiler named Abe who "sees dead people." The October 30, 2003, article said that the psychic pooch accompanied the folks with Seven Paranormal Research to haunted sites, where he sensed spirits. According to the report, when the investigators searched Fort Fisher, a Confederate fort by the mouth of the Cape Fear River, Abe nudged a researcher's hand and went into pointing mode. All eyes looked to see what he was pointing at and witnessed a fully developed apparition standing atop a mound.

It seemed to be life imitating art with Abe accompanying a paranormal research team just as his cartoon counterpart does in *Scooby-Doo!*

Seven Paranormal Research, stationed in Carthage, North Carolina, appeared on a Learning Channel television special that showed off Abe's skills.

𝕮𝖍𝖔𝖘𝖙𝖘 𝖎𝖓 𝖙𝖍𝖊 𝕹𝖊𝖜𝖘

Lighthouse Cat

OHIO'S HISTORIC FAIRPORT HARBOR LIGHTHOUSE, a fixture on the shores of Lake Erie, has long been the source of ghost stories. It was said to be home to the spirit of a gray cat but local skeptics laughed at the stories of the lighthouse volunteers. The lighthouse folks had the last laugh when their claims gained legitimacy because of a recent gruesome discovery.

A vintage photograph of the Fairport Harbor Lighthouse, where a ghostly cat makes its home. (Courtesy of the Fairport Harbor Historical Society)

On May 26, 2001, Cleveland's newspaper, the *Plain Dealer,* reported that "workers installing air conditioning vents discovered the mummified remains of a gray cat in a crawl space."

Curator Pamela Brent insisted that she'd seen "the wispy gray spirit of a cat" several times. The report quoted her as saying, "It would skitter across the floor near the kitchen, like it was playing. I would catch glimpses of it from time to time. Then one evening I felt its presence when it jumped on the bed. I felt its weight pressing on me."

Vindicated by the discovery of the kitty, the folks at the lighthouse further investigated and discovered that a former lighthouse keeper's wife did indeed have pet cats. Bedridden because of illness, Mary Babcock occupied the second floor, where her cats kept her company and brought her comfort. Mary died of arteriosclerosis (a thickening of the arterial walls) when she was close to seventy, but no one knows how the cat met its demise.

The Fairport Harbor Marine Museum and Lighthouse draws many tourists who say the sixty-nine-step trip up to the top is worth it for the sweeping view of Lake Erie. Located approximately twenty-five miles northeast of Cleveland, Ohio, the museum displays many fascinating artifacts. In addition to showcasing its maritime exhibits, the lighthouse tour includes a peek at the cat's mummy—something that particularly fascinates schoolchildren on field trips, who also have their eyes peeled for a friendly kitty ghost!

FAIRPORT HARBOR MARINE MUSEUM AND LIGHTHOUSE
129 SECOND STREET
FAIRPORT HARBOR, OH 44077
(440) 354-4825

Spirit Photography Capturing Ghosts

Seeing is believing. That old adage is true. Many people who once doubted the existence of ghosts become firm believers once their own eyes witness the evidence.

Surveys show that about one in eight Americans admit they have actually seen a ghost. The majority of folks must rely on the accounts of others to convince them. This is difficult for many skeptics who need proof before they believe. Little actual evidence of the existence of ghosts has been found. We must depend on the reports of credible witnesses. Yet there is one startling type of evidence that leaves skeptics slack-jawed.

Photographs.

The following pages showcase photos that I believe have captured ghosts. Can I say absolutely that they are not fakes? No. I wasn't there when these pictures were taken. I can, however, vouch for the characters of the photographers mentioned here. In my quest for true ghost photos, I interviewed many folks who claimed to have captured ghosts on film. In my final selection of spirit pictures, I looked for the most startling images taken by sincere people. Indeed, it took some cajoling for some of them to allow me to publicize their work.

Little Joe

Wally. Uncle Wally. Beasty. Booty Girl. Turtle. Piggy Piggy. Sister Smudge. Amber. Snickers. Little Joe.

Before they found refuge in Anita Morris's Portland, Oregon, backyard sanctuary, these ten beautiful felines lived the hard life of America's millions of feral cats.

Feral cats are simply cats born without homes and not tamed by humans. They seek shelter in places like abandoned buildings and over-grown blackberry bushes. They live on rodents and garbage pail scraps. Unprotected, their lives are often short, but the population continues to grow as they breed. And breed. And breed.

Anita first became aware of the feral cat dilemma when an elderly wheelchair-bound neighbor began feeding a couple of stray cats. Not spayed or neutered, the cats bred and before too long, over one hundred cats were swarming the neighborhood. It tugged at Anita's heartstrings to see the scrawny, homeless creatures. "I got involved with the Feral Cat Coalition of Oregon," explained Anita, a grandmother of five.

She began trapping the strays in the humane Have a Heart Traps and got them spayed and neutered. Nineteen years later, she is still doing her part to help the hapless kitties. In fact, she and her husband, Joe, have turned their backyard into an oasis for feral cats, complete with cozy little houses.

While most feral cats are wary of humans and won't let them close, one special cat won Anita's heart and she won his. Little Joe was a big white and gray boy with a little dot beneath his nose. He loved to play with the humans. "He liked to fetch acorns," she remembered fondly.

They nicknamed him "the Mayor" because he always welcomed new cats. Whenever a strange cat wandered into the yard, Little Joe would eagerly greet him and then show him to the food dish. "It was like he was saying, 'This is a great place! Look, they have food and toys!'" Anita smiled at the memory but her eyes saddened as she told me of Little Joe's tragic end. He was hit by a car and she and her husband were devastated as they prepared to bury him. "I wish we had gotten a picture of him," she lamented. As they looked around at the surviving cats, they realized they had no photos of any of them. "We rushed out and got some film."

Anita got out her Olympus camera and took a roll of pictures of her backyard kitties. When she and Joe went to pick up the photos, they sat in their car and looked over the snapshots. Suddenly, Anita gasped. And then they both started crying. For there, smack in the middle of a photo, was the undeniable image of Little Joe. He sat behind the food trough, between Amber and Booty Girl.

Little Joe is slightly transparent, allowing the lines of the shed behind him to show through his body. But other than that, he appears just as he did in life.

I learned of the extraordinary photo (taken with ordinary film) through a friend of Anita's and it took some coaxing for her to allow me to include her story in this book. "I don't want Little Joe to be exploited," Anita insisted.

"Little Joe's story will help a lot of people feel better," I told her. "It will comfort them to see his picture and to know that their pets' spirits live on."

She finally agreed to allow me to use the amazing image of the cat's ghost. "I'd like the best possible print," I told her. "It would be better if you could have one made from the original negative, rather than a copy."

(Third from left, the slightly transparent white and gray kitty standing up behind the food dish) The spirit of Little Joe appears beside his friends. (Anita Morris)

Anita misunderstood and when she couldn't find the negative sent the photo to Kodak to have a new negative made. She soon received a phone call from a puzzled Kodak employee. "There's a problem with the photo," said the woman.

"Oh?" Anita replied.

"The cat is transparent," said the woman.

"Yes," said Anita.

"He looks like a ghost!" said the woman.

A picture tells a thousand stories.

For information on feral cats, visit www.feralcats.com.

Say Cheese

"What a waste of money!" said Jude Huff-Felz when she looked through the envelope of just-printed photographs. She and her mother had gone on a ghost-hunting expedition with Dale Kaczmarek of the Ghost Research Society in Illinois.

Jude had indulged in a roll of expensive infrared film—the temperature-sensitive film that ghost enthusiasts often use to capture apparitions. The group had visited the infamous Bachelor's Grove Cemetery in Chicago, Illinois, on a summer day in 1991. Established in 1864, the old cemetery was rumored to have once been a dumping site for gangsters' victims, and accounts of ghost sightings there are overwhelming.

"Dale had us go through the cemetery in pairs, while the rest of the group waited," Jude said. "My mom and I walked through together. In one place I stood there and turned in a circle, taking a photo from every angle."

The resulting photographs, at first, seemed unremarkable. But as Jude looked through them again, she gasped. There, off to the side of one picture, was the distinctive figure of a person sitting atop a grave. "I didn't notice it at first because it was on the edge of the picture," she told me.

She and her mom are both positive there was no one there when the photographs were taken—no one but a *ghost,* that is!

Though Jude's amazing photograph was featured in the *Chicago Sun,* and in several ghost books, and can be found on various Web sites, she is not getting rich or famous. In fact, until this writer offered her a modest fee to use the photo, no one had offered or paid her so much as a nickel. It never occurred to her to try to make money from something she simply found fascinating.

Jude Huff-Felz thought she had wasted her money on infrared film, until she looked closely at this photograph and realized she had captured a ghost sitting upon a grave. (See the left side of the photograph.) (Jude Huff-Felz)

Violet

Joe Jones, owner of a motorcycle-towing business in Vista, California, has a most unusual hobby. He photographs ghosts and has a Web site devoted to the topic.

The art comes naturally to Joe, who admits to a strong intuition—a sixth sense that some parapsychologists believe makes capturing ghosts on film natural. Some theorize that simply having a sensitive nearby while taking pictures increases the odds of photographing an ethereal being.

Joe used infrared film while photographing the haunted Whaley House in Old Town San Diego. (Readers of *Coast to Coast Ghosts* will remember that Violet Whaley committed suicide there in the late 1880s.) The man peering into the window is Joe's very much alive friend. The woman passing behind the column is from "the other side."

The ghost of a woman emerges from behind a column on the porch of the Whaley House. (Joe Jones)

Ghosts in the News

WITNESSES SAID THE VICTIM of a fatal car wreck in Oklahoma City materialized in Puckett's Wrecker Yard and was caught on videotape, according to Oklahoma City's Channel Four News. The ABC-TV station aired the footage, which showed a milky, human-shaped figure circling above a wrecked car.

Tracy Martin, a thirty-three-year-old mother of twins, died on June 30, 2002, and her family believes that it was her spirit that made national news with its startling appearance eighteen days later in the wrecker yard where her truck was towed.

Overnight dispatcher Kathy Henley watched the scene live from a monitor and was startled at the sight of a specter circling above wrecked vehicles and peeking in windows as if looking for something. An employee sent outside to investigate found nothing unusual but when the video was replayed there was no explaining the ghostly image.

Though there were other vehicles there that had been involved in fatal accidents and the somewhat cloudy apparition did not have distinctive features, Tracy Martin's family asserted the spirit had to be her, as she always "did things in grand style" and they were certain she wanted them to know she was okay. Tracy's twins were shown the video by their father, who hoped it would bring them some comfort.

This story, garnered from a number of news sources, was broken by the Oklahoma City Channel Four News, July 2002.

Ghostly Letters

"I've never told anyone this before because I'm afraid people will think I'm crazy . . ."

That is the way the letters often begin. I get them every day from people all over the world who have seen ghosts. The experiences have left them awestruck, amazed, excited, or frightened. They are not sure if they can trust their own eyes. The world they knew—or *thought* they knew—was turned inside out for a surreal moment they will never forget. They need to tell *someone*.

After reading this author's *Coast to Coast Ghosts: True Stories of Hauntings Across America,* they decide that I am one person who *will* believe them. And I do.

Sometimes they simply need reassurance. Sometimes they need advice. And sometimes they simply want to tell their stories.

With the writers' permission, I've chosen a few of these letters to share with you. Here is a peek into my mailbag!

Phantom Stalker
From Kellie Martin

I am 20 yrs. old, and live in Springdale, Arkansas. When I was a little girl, about ten or eleven years old, we lived in a house that I could have sworn was haunted by some force. I wasn't sure what it was, and I hadn't seen anything, but I had that gut feeling.

I slept with my bedroom door cracked. One night, I looked in the shadowed area between my door and the wall. I saw a man standing there, and it freaked me out. To this day I remember exactly what he looked like and exactly what he was wearing. He was an older man, with a bald spot on top, and a white ring of hair around that bald spot. He was about 5'9" and he was wearing a red and black, long-sleeve flannel shirt; along with a pair of blue jeans. He just stood there and watched me, until I got the nerve to get up and turn on my lamp. When I did so, he was no longer there. The man in my room had disappeared, leading me to believe that my room, if not my whole house, was haunted.

I never told anybody about what I had seen because I was afraid that they would make fun, or that they wouldn't believe me at all. I didn't even tell my own sister about it. She is a year and a half older than I.

Now, the odd thing is that about a year after I saw the man in my room, my sister came home from school, and she was freaked out. I asked her what was wrong. She said, "I was in the bathroom after school, waiting for Mom to pick me up. I was fixing my hair in the mirror, and in the bathroom stall behind me was a man standing there watching me. I thought it was the janitor so I turned around to leave. When I turned around, he wasn't there."

I asked my sister what he looked like, and she said, "He was about 6' tall, with a bald head, but with a little bit of white hair around the bottom of his head. He was wearing a red and black, long-sleeve flannel shirt with jeans."

When I heard this, I about flipped out. I was very scared. I asked her what he was doing, and she told me that he was just watching her. I told her that I had seen the same man in my bedroom about a year before.

Do you think he could be my guardian angel? Is it possible that my sister and I have the same one?

Author's Note:
Though no one can say for certain who the apparition was, my guess is he was not an angel. Angel experts insist that people who encounter them are never frightened but left with an overwhelming sense of peace.

In further communication, Kellie said that the man did not resemble any deceased family members that she was aware of. It is possible that the ghost seen by Kellie and her sister originated from either the school or their home and followed them to the other place. Perhaps the Martin sisters resembled someone he was attached to in life.

Special Child
(ANONYMOUS UPON REQUEST)

I am the mother of an autistic son. I have never before talked about the experiences I have had with my son, for fear that somebody might think I am insane. I will do my best to describe what happened.

The first incident occurred long before Nathan* was diagnosed with autism. He was an incredibly intelligent baby, yet did not speak a word, though it appeared he was inventing his own language. He seemed to have some kind of relationship with walls. He would stare at the walls and laugh hysterically. He seemed to be watching a silent, invisible movie. One day he stood very close to the wall and whispered unintelligible words from his own language. Then he put his finger over his mouth and said, "Shhh."

This was very unusual because he did not interact with anybody *ever* for any reason. He had never made the shushing noise before.

---

* Whenever an asterisk appears, names have been changed to protect privacy.

At first I wrote this off as autistic behavior, but then I began to wonder if Nathan was interacting with a world the rest of us couldn't see.

Nathan was something of a savant—displaying extraordinary mental agility, as autistic children sometimes do. He knew things he should not know. He could count, instantly add and subtract without use of words, numbers, or symbols. Though I am a math whiz, my son seemed to have some kind of *magic* with numbers.

But he also appeared to sense things, long before the rest of us. Each morning of the day we were to visit my family, Nathan vomited. *Every* time. For years.

The "coincidence" here is that my family has since disowned me. They did not approve of the fact I refused to send Nathan away because of his autism. They could not accept what they perceived to be a flaw in him. Nathan always seemed to have some kind of ESP, and I wonder if he knew they hated him for being autistic.

One of Nathan's aides at school witnessed an occurrence of ESP. She had put some jelly beans in her desk drawer before he arrived. She said that he walked in that morning and immediately went into the drawer and grabbed the jelly beans. She was shocked, as no one else knew the candy was there and Nathan broke his normal routine to go to the drawer—something unheard of with autistic people.

One of the most incredible things occurred when we moved into our cottage five years ago. One morning Nathan motioned for me to come into his room. He pointed at the wall where the light switch is. I thought he wanted the light on, so I told him he could turn it on. He then took my hand and we walked into the bathroom, where he got a small piece of toilet paper and handed it to me. Then he motioned for me to go back to his room with him. He looked at the same spot on his wall and said, "Ghost is crying."

He motioned for me to wipe away tears with toilet paper. Nervous, I laughed. He repeated, "Ghost is crying."

I decided to wipe away the tears and he seemed satisfied.

I was baffled, as this was completely contradictory to his behavior. He does not talk that way. He does not behave that way. He doesn't have an abstract imagination. I admit that it freaked me out. A few minutes later I went back to his room and tried to ask him about it. As usual, there was no reaction to my words.

How could he know how to console someone if he could not accept it from me?

Author's Note:
The autistic mind is somewhat of a mystery. Not lacking in intelligence, the special people afflicted with this malady think differently from the rest of us. Challenged to communicate with others, they often have extraordinary abilities superior to "normal" people. A correlation between autism and ESP along with the ability to see ghosts has been noted. Nathan's mother hopes that serious research will be done on this connection, and her story has been passed along to paranormal researcher Dr. Sally Rhine Feather, Director of Development at the Rhine Research Center in Durham, North Carolina.

Last Words
FROM YANULA MINI

I am working up the nerve to tell you of a very strange experience I had in Washington, D.C., many years ago. When I was sixteen, I went out East to participate in a program to study Congress. As the only liberal in a group of fifty teenagers, I tended to get ganged up on in debates. During one particularly lively debate on Social Security, I got pushed over a chair, spraining my ankle.

The emergency room was busy, so I was placed in a curtained-off area to wait until a doctor was available. The curtain next to me opened slightly, and I saw another teenager on a gurney, crying. I could see that she was a very pretty black girl, despite the fact her face and chest had been cut so badly. She'd evidently lost a lot of blood. Her face was pale and her eyes stared as if she couldn't focus. I asked her what was wrong, and she told me about a ghastly rape at knifepoint. Still crying, she rolled over and went to sleep.

Eventually, a nurse came in to see me. "Will Sharon be all right?" I asked, angry that she had been left alone when she was clearly in so much pain. Looking startled, the nurse asked me what I was talking about. I told her that I had been chatting with the girl, and she had told me all about her rape.

Very much to the nurse's credit, she believed me. Since I could not walk at the time, there was no question of my having gone into the next cubicle to read Sharon's chart. She also did not tell me that the girl had died twenty minutes before I arrived and was no longer in the adjacent cubicle. I found that out later, after the nurse had fetched a police officer.

To this day, I do not know if the nurse told the officer when I had the conversation with Sharon. I suspect not. The officer listened very seriously to my account of what Sharon had said, which included many details about her attackers. He took notes and asked me follow-up questions, exactly as if I had been a witness to Sharon's dying declaration.

After the officer left and I was bandaged up, the nurse took me out into the waiting area in a wheelchair. Just before we exited the emergency room, she whispered in my ear that we should keep my seeing Sharon's spirit as our little secret. It was not until that moment that I realized that Sharon was a ghost.

In response to my frightened questions, the nurse said this was not the first time that she had seen a murder victim's spirit hang around to testify, and Sharon was lucky to have found someone who could hear her so quickly.

I do not know if the police ever caught Sharon's attackers. I was certainly never contacted to testify. I imagine that the officer would have had a hard time reconciling the hospital records of when she died with when I arrived. I do know, however, that I was correct about where her various wounds were, because the officer checked my account against a drawing in her chart. And I am positive that Sharon wanted her story told.

Other than talking with the police officer, I have kept this as a secret between me and the nurse for all of these years. I have reservations about passing it along at all, because one wouldn't want to touch off a spate of emergency room victims making things up about one another.

Yet if this is a common type of spirit appearance, I am surprised that I've never seen or heard a similar story.

Dangerous Games
FROM LOIS WREN

Twelve years ago my husband and I moved into half of an old Victorian duplex in Cleveland Heights, Ohio. From the beginning, the place gave me the creeps. Doors would inexplicably open and close and footsteps echoed in the empty hallways. I'd also experience rushes of cold air. My engineer husband would always have some logical explanation for the occurrences.

Many mornings when I was alone and my husband had gone to work I would clearly hear, "Edith!* Edith!" in a plaintive, childlike voice. It frightened me so much that I started to leave the house several hours early so as not to be alone.

On Halloween *nobody* came to our house. We were baffled as we watched the children cross the street to avoid our home.

Finally I did some research and found a magazine and a newspaper article reporting on a death from twelve years before. A woman named Marion Walls* plunged to her death from the attic of our house!

Her husband told the police that she had been hanging curtains when the accident occurred. Yet, she had been naked and her ankles and wrists were bound. The paperboy and neighbors had come forward to report that Mr. and Mrs. Walls played strange games and that they had seen her dangling from the attic window before. Until the accident, Mr. Walls had

---

* Whenever an asterisk appears, names have been changed to protect privacy.

always managed to rescue her by pulling her into the window from the floor below.

I checked and saw that there were indeed dents on the windowsill apparently made by rope burns. Browsing the old obituaries, I found that the viewing of Marion's body was held in the parlor of our house and was hosted by her sister, *Edith*.

There were many incidents during our year in that house and even my straight-laced, black and white, engineer husband came to believe that Marion's ghost was there. When we moved out I told the landlord about it and he said, "Oh, my wife divorced me after we moved here. She always got the creeps in that house."

Prior to our moving out, the man in the other half of the duplex made an annoyed comment to my husband about "all the racket last night."

We'd heard it too and assumed it was *them* having a party. He also mentioned hearing people running up and down the stairs, which we had heard as well. Needless to say, we were pleased to get out of there.

Old Woman
From Donna Palacsko

My husband and I went to a restaurant in Canada called Ed's. It is about a one-hundred-year-old house that has now turned into a very famous Calgary landmark restaurant.

Something very strange happened to me while I was heading up the stairs to the washroom. On my way up, I found myself behind an old lady who appeared to be in her eighties. She was moving very slowly. Her gnarled hand grasped the handrail as she inched her way up. I did not want her to feel rushed so I stayed a couple of stair steps behind her. She finally made it to the top and we both headed for the washroom. I reached in front of her to open the door, and she entered before me. She never turned to look at me at any time.

The old woman ambled into the first stall as I went to a mirror to put on my lipstick. I washed my hands, fixed my hair, and applied more lipstick. Then I realized that there were no noises coming from the stall the old lady had entered.

Worried, I pretended to fix my boot and peeked under the stall to see if she was okay. No one was there.

I opened the door to the stall and was stunned to find it empty. I could not have missed seeing her leave.

I quickly left the washroom and found three waitresses folding napkins. I asked them if they had seen the old lady. None of them had so I rushed downstairs and asked the hostess if she knew where the old lady had gone.

The hostess had not seen the woman, but she had a knowing look in her eyes. The place was haunted, she told me, and explained that many odd things happened there.

I always thought that a ghost would be transparent and that I would be really freaked out if I saw one.

If this truly was a ghost, she seemed to be unaware of the people around her. She was able to touch things and not go *through* them. I believe I saw a ghost and consequently am no longer afraid of them.

Nantucket Ghost
FROM SUSAN BEAUPRE KISH

In January 1992, I bought a little house on Nantucket Island, off the coast of Cape Cod. I uprooted myself from Boston and got a job in a hotel and real estate company. My family helped me move one stormy weekend. They stayed one night with me and left the next day. I had a good day unpacking my things and settling in. I fell into bed exhausted at the end of the day, listening to the wind howling around the house and the foghorn blowing in the harbor. In the middle of the night, I saw an old woman standing over me, bending down and staring at me. I started screaming and I guess I would have to say woke up, but the vision was so real it didn't seem like I was sleeping. The sounds of my screams echoed off the walls because I hadn't had a chance to put any curtains up to muffle sound.

The next morning I met my next-door neighbor. I told her I had seen a ghost in the house. My neighbor, a very practical woman, said, "Oh, did she have gray hair?" To which I replied, "Yes."

Then she asked, "Was she wearing a housedress?"

Yes again!

My neighbor replied, "Oh, don't worry, that was Virginia. She owned the house before you. She and her husband bought it as a retirement home but then he died before they moved here. His ashes are buried in the yard under the cherry tree. When she died, she was buried in New Jersey, near her daughters. All you have to do is tell her that you love the house and will take care of it and the tree."

Well, I thought it was a little odd but I said those words aloud that night and didn't see the ghost again.

Four months later I rented the second bedroom to a summer worker who had answered an ad I placed on the town bulletin board. Her first night there I woke up to screams and ran out into the living room at the same time she did. She shouted, "I just saw an old lady in my room!"

I asked her if she had gray hair and wore a housedress and she said yes. I told her to tell her she loved the house and would take care of it and the tree. She went back to her room and followed my instructions.

We never saw Virginia again.

Author's Note:
Though Susan Beaupre Kish now lives in Switzerland, she still visits Nantucket. She reports that her former home has been sold and enlarged. Whenever she is in the area, she stops by the cherry tree to pay her respects to Virginia's husband.

Restless Ghost
FROM ANITA PORTERFIELD

Imagine a small rock house resting 2,200 feet up on the side of a hill. The view is immense and spectacular. Massive oak trees and dense cedar brush provide a natural barrier to what most of us think of as civilization. The isolation is not total, however. One can see a sprinkling of houses within the thick vegetation. Now imagine a bitter old man and his disagreeable daughter in alcoholic rages shouting and threatening to kill one another. The neighbors frequently call the Kendall County Sheriff's Department to intervene in these violent skirmishes. Several times a year an ambulance pulls in the driveway, retrieves the old man, and hauls him off to the Kerrville VA Hospital to dry out. This is their way of life. These are the people who lived in our house before us.

Hard freezes are uncommon in South Texas. Ice storms are a rarity. My husband, John, and I began our move to Boerne one icy January day in 1997. We had not closed on our mortgage loan, but the executor of the estate that owned the house gave us permission to begin moving in.

We moved a U-Haul load over on a frigid Saturday afternoon; I stayed at the new place and John went back to the old house to get another load. The bad weather worsened. A terrible ice storm began and he couldn't make it back. I was in the new house alone with no heat and no telephone. John had built a fire in the fireplace and had left a few small logs but neither one of us had expected to stay the night. After cleaning the kitchen cupboards and lining them with paper, I began unpacking boxes. The weather worsened again and I could hear ice being pelted up against the house. I instinctively knew that there was no way that John could make it back. I ate a can of tuna and lay down exhausted on a mattress in the master bedroom. I had a small radio and turned it on, more for the noise than anything else. After a few minutes I heard noises from the kitchen. I went to look and all of the cupboard doors were open. Being somewhat compulsive in nature, I closed them and hurried back to the mattress. Again I heard noises. Once more I got up and once more the cupboard doors were open. I knew that I had closed them. A light came on in the laundry room and I got scared. A few minutes later the light went off in the laundry room and one came on in the master bath. The door between the laundry room and bathroom slammed shut. I ran to another bedroom. I knew that I was going to be killed that night. The pattern repeated itself. This time I heard the cabinet doors open and close. More lights came on in the laundry room. Lights went off in the bathroom. I noticed that the area of activity was confined to those places. By daybreak I was certain that I had experienced a restless ghost. My husband arrived shortly thereafter. He was skeptical.

Monday morning at the closing, the lady at the title company asked us if we knew that the previous owner had committed suicide in the house. I looked at John and said, "I told you there was a ghost in that house!"

The ghost made his presence known almost every night. I guess we just became accustomed to him. As time passed, the living and the dead coexisted with little notice. For reasons that I won't go into here, several months after we moved in we sued the estate that had owned the house. The executor was the ghost's sister. She informed us that she was dying of lung cancer. The ghost's son lived in Florida and was dying of AIDS. Our certified letter to the ghost's daughter was returned. She had committed suicide a few days before our letter to her was mailed. Our ghost was gone. We last heard him on the day of his daughter's death.

A few months later I was on a ladder stripping wallpaper off the master bathroom walls and over the doorway I noticed some odd-looking stains. They were brown and appeared to be splatters. I was certain that I was looking at bloodstains. I called John into the room and after looking closely, he came to the same conclusion. We also came to the horrible realization that those splatters were most likely not from a self-inflicted wound.

One day in conversation with one of our neighbors, I mentioned something about our ghost's suicide. He told me that the sheriff's department had investigated the death and had come to the conclusion that it was a homicide and that the daughter was their number-one suspect. They had not been able to prove their suspicions.

I know that what we experienced was a ghost. I also know that he has not been back since the death of his daughter. And, yes, I feel in my heart that she killed him.

Author's Note:
Anita Porterfield writes that her home is now a peaceful place. Reports of paranormal activity surrounding places of murder or suicide are common. When the alleged killer finally died, her victim may have been freed from the need to avenge his death. Or did her spirit manage to evolve and rescue his? Perhaps she came for him so they could resolve their conflicts and move peacefully into the afterlife.

Nightmare House
FROM LISA DUCKWORTH

I still have nightmares about a rental house I lived in over thirty years ago. When we moved into the Little Rock, Arkansas, house in 1972, it felt a little strange but we put it down to a change in scenery. My mother was disabled and newly divorced, so things *were* a bit strange. Then one Friday night, my sister Laura, myself, and my mother were in the front bathroom. Mom was brushing her teeth and Laura was sitting cross-legged on the toilet, and I was perched on the side of the bathtub. We were discussing our dates with Mom, telling her about what was going on in our lives. It was around 10:30 P.M.

We heard something in the dining room. (You could see across the hall into the dining room from the bathroom.) My mom looked toward the noise and got a funny expression on her face, so we looked too. We saw a woman who bore a striking resemblance to my older sister, Marion (now deceased).

She was tall, blonde, a little pale, and was wearing a long white nightgown and was barefooted. She looked like she was floating about a foot off the floor. My mom asked what she wanted and she turned her head and looked at us and then went through the French doors into the living room.

We just sat there, numb.

As months went by, several others saw ghosts in our home. There were two that seemed to "live there." One was the blonde woman, who appeared to be in her mid-twenties and stood approximately 5'9–10". She stayed in the front of the house in the dining room and living room area. There was also an older man. He had dark hair, was bearded, and appeared angry. Just his upper torso would appear.

There was a back room that felt so creepy that all of us avoided it, friends and family alike. We later found out the house had a reputation for people moving out in the middle of the night. We lasted about seven or eight months.

To this day, the house is still the only rental house on the block. I know it sounds crazy, but many people saw apparitions there. It was not a group hysteria thing, as we had guests that came to visit—with no idea of what was going on—leave literally screaming in the night.

We never said a lot about it to our neighbors. They would have thought we were all crazy. The house is like a bad dream.

My husband and I drove by the house the other day. It still looks the same. It was built up on a small hill and is all dark red brick with a big front porch. The back butts up to an alley. It looks perfectly ordinary, but inside the place you can feel how creepy it really is.

Author's Note:
As Lisa and I corresponded about the nightmare house from her past, we both grew more curious. She proved to be a diligent researcher, digging up information on the history of the home. She found that the house was built in 1925 and she acquired a long list of the home's occupants.

Lisa noted that the first owners of the home were a young couple—the

bride just twenty-six. Interestingly, the woman died in November 1972, just
months after Lisa's family moved into the rental.

A common theory among paranormal investigators is that ghosts can appear
in the shape of their former selves at any age. If this is the case, then perhaps
the ghost was drawn back to her first home and appeared as she did when she
lived there in the 1920s.

It is also possible that the ghosts belonged to people who lived in a differ-
ent house built at that location long before 1925.

Who was the angry man—and why *was he so angry? Lisa Duckworth*
and I are still curious and she continues her research into the mysteries of the
Little Rock house.

Curtain Call

Theaters are notoriously haunted. Almost every old theater seems to
claim a ghost or two. What is it about them that makes them so haunted?
Is it the extreme emotion of the actors that attracts ethereal beings?

That is one theory. But it is not just the theaters that feature stage
productions that swirl with paranormal phenomena. Old movie theaters, too, are home to ghosts.

Perhaps it is the fact that the configuration of theaters rarely
changes that makes them candidates for hauntings. The rows of seats are
anchored and the aisles cut permanent paths beside them.

This writer has noticed an unusual number of ghost sightings in
old places where furniture is not moved and the environment is unal-
tered. (Old restrooms and staircases are also good examples of this phenomenon. Ghost sightings are frequent here too.)

Perhaps when the physical setting doesn't change, the energy from
past events remains intact. Perhaps it takes a sort of cosmic sweeping—
a rearranging of the environment—to release this energy.

Or maybe when the space is not rearranged it is so familiar to a
stuck soul that they have trouble realizing that things have indeed
changed and it is time to move on.

Whatever the reason, there are haunted theaters all over the world,
including the following:

Working Overtime

Florida's Tampa Theatre, opened in 1926, is said to be home to a man who died there. He was the projectionist for decades until his death at the theater in the 1960s. This ornate movie palace, decked out in Florida Mediterranean style, is on the National Register of Historic Places. Over 150,000 people enjoy films and concerts there each year. The man, who perished in the projection booth, is thought to be responsible for the odd occurrences there, including the inexplicable sound of jingling keys and the moving of objects from place to place. Some report that they feel his phantom fingers caress their necks.

TAMPA THEATRE

711 FRANKLIN STREET

TAMPA, FL 33602

(813) 274-8286

WWW.TAMPATHEATRE.ORG

Still Hanging Around

The Rialto Theater in Winslow, Arizona, has long been legendary as a haunted hot spot. Once an opera house, it has seen its share of drama on and off the stage.

A ghostly lady appears on a balcony, where she allegedly hung herself. Employees have reported hearing laughter and conversation emanating from the first row of the empty theater seats when the Rialto is closed. The thick, flowery scent of vintage perfume wafts through the air in the old dressing rooms despite the fact they have not been used for half a century.

RIALTO THEATER

115 WEST KINSLEY STREET

WINSLOW, AZ 86047

(928) 289-4100

Imprints

Mann's Chinese Theater (once known as Grauman's Chinese Theater) opened its doors in 1927 and has been a Hollywood landmark ever since.

Rising ninety feet high, the bronze roof has patinaed to a lovely shade of jade. Tourists from around the world visit its sidewalk. It is here that stars left their prints in wet cement. This tradition began as an accident when silent screen actress Normal Talmadge stumbled into some wet cement and left her print. While over two hundred stars have left their mark outside of the theater, several mysterious presences have left their mark *inside*. It is here that witnesses say that phantom hands yank on the stage curtain and play pranks on people in the dressing rooms. Some credit the haunting to actor Victor Kilian, who was viciously murdered nearby in 1976.

MANN'S CHINESE THEATER
6925 HOLLYWOOD BOULEVARD
HOLLYWOOD, CA 90028
(323) 464-8111

Encore

The original Rhode Opera House in Kenosha, Wisconsin, was built in 1891, several blocks from Lake Michigan. Damaged by fire five years later, it was rebuilt on the same spot and folks have been gathering there to be entertained ever since. In addition to showcasing live performances, it has also served as a movie theater.

Today it is home to the Lakeside Players, a community theater group that is dedicated to enthralling audiences. They make no secret about the fact there are ghosts in their midst. In addition to hearing phantom piano music and disembodied laughter, witnesses report seeing a transparent man running between rows of seats, and sitting in a seat near the back of the theater.

A child was reportedly visiting backstage when she suddenly exclaimed about the beautiful ladies. The baffled adults asked her to explain and she described women in long gowns that only she could see.

RHODE OPERA HOUSE
514 FIFTY-SIXTH STREET
KENOSHA, WI 53140
(262) 657-PLAY (7529)
WWW.RHODEOPERA.COM

eight

Their House Is a Museum

Museums, usually housed in old mansions or historic buildings and filled with artifacts of the past, are naturals as haunted places. Sometimes the ghosts belong to family members or servants who once lived in the house. And sometimes the ghosts are unwittingly donated to the museum along with a piece of antique furniture. (Yes, ghosts have been known to be attached to an old bed or a dresser as well as to a building!)

While some curators are tight-lipped about the ghostly activity in their museums, others realize that a reputation as a haunted place is a boon for business and are enthusiastic about sharing their stories. The following are a few fascinating museums where visitors sometimes see ghosts:

Mordecai House

It was a sunny autumn morning in Raleigh, North Carolina, when Teri Jones stopped by the Mordecai House to check on the progress of the workmen.

The lovely family home–turned–museum was under renovation and a new man was on the job. Teri stepped into the spacious foyer and looked up to see the man atop a ladder. His hands shook as he spread the plaster on the ceiling. His face ashen, he asked, "Were you here a few minutes ago?"

"No," she replied. "I just got here. Why?"

He shook his head as if he could not believe his own words as he described the odd visit by a woman in an old-fashioned dress.

Teri smiled knowingly as he pointed through the French doors to the stairway beyond. "She came down the stairs," he said. "And then she opened the French doors and walked into the hallway. She turned around and shut the doors behind her and then walked into that room." He gestured toward the dining room.

Curious, but not alarmed, the man had climbed from his ladder and followed her. "But there was no one there!" he said.

He had just met the Mordecai ghost.

Teri, the Mordecai House site manager since 1996, knew the man wasn't pulling her leg. "He'd never been here before and knew nothing about the history of the house," she explained. "I questioned him very carefully." The unsuspecting workman had just described the exact scenario that had been witnessed at least once before.

Twenty years earlier, in fact, a housekeeper named Rosa had seen the apparition of a lady in a long dress sweep down the old staircase. The description matched that of Mary Mordecai as she had appeared in her younger days, and the assumption is made that the ghost belongs to her.

As do many of us, Mary grew less attractive in her senior years and was apparently insulted when, in another incident, some visitors made fun of her picture, which was on display in an upstairs bedroom. For as they laughed and made an unkind comment about her, the picture suddenly toppled over—though it had been securely placed and no one was near it.

Mordecai House, built in the 1780s, had once been the heart of one of the biggest antebellum plantations in Wake County with thousands of acres of wheat, corn, and sweet potatoes. In business during a shameful time for our country, the Mordecai family had many slaves who worked the land and waited on them. In fact, the bell used to call them to serve the meals still hangs outside the dining room window.

The grounds remain lush and green with enormous broad-leaf trees creating welcome shade on hot days. St. Mark's Chapel, where two hundred couples are wed each year, and the humble home where the seventeenth president, Andrew Johnson, was born, now also share the land.

Mordecai House is an imposing structure with big shuttered windows and graceful balconies. "Five generations of the same family lived here up until 1968," Teri said as she pointed out various pieces of original furniture. Paintings, photographs, and personal possessions also fill the rooms, lending an almost chilling sense of continuity to the grand atmosphere. It's as if a little piece of each person who ever lived there still remains.

Some of the children's toys occupy upstairs bedrooms—including an unfortunate dolly whose face bears the results of a long ago game of hospital. "A little boy was determined to give her her medicine," Teri replied when asked about the large hole punched between the doll's eyes.

The chill felt at Mordecai House goes beyond the sense of history. Puzzling cold spots have been measured in the downstairs parlor. Part of

Mordecai House is still home to the long-dead Mordecai family. (Leslie Rule)

the original structure, it had once been the center of activity in the home. "We can't explain it," Teri said, describing how a climate-controlled heating system was installed to protect the museum's precious artifacts. The system was designed to moderate temperatures in the entire house.

Yet the mysterious icy spots persist. In addition to experiencing the baffling cold spots, *this* writer felt something else.

I was on a private tour with Lynette Minnich, the librarian from the Rhine Research Center, and we followed Teri upstairs. After admiring the lovely rooms there, I sat down next to Teri in the hallway upon the worn wood floors. Suddenly I was startled by the unmistakable sensation of a tug on the back of my shirt.

"I just felt something tug on my shirt," I said.

"I didn't do it," said Teri.

Of course she didn't. She was three feet away from me. Lynette was standing six feet away.

While I would much rather have *seen* Mary, or any other ghost who may inhabit the spacious house, I will have to be satisfied with that simple mysterious sensation.

On Lynette's prior visit she and a few staff members from the Rhine Research Center had been invited to see the mansion. They were gathered with Teri in the same upstairs hallway when they heard a sudden, urgent pounding on the front door. Teri hurried downstairs and opened the door but the huge yard was empty. Perhaps it was simply someone playing a prank, but the timing was odd, as they had been discussing ghosts.

Since my April 2003 visit to Mordecai House, Teri reported that paranormal activity has escalated. "A new employee went to work for us," she told me. "She is extremely sensitive and has heard a female voice calling her name. Something happens almost every day. They're mostly little things, but they are things we can't explain."

In October 2003, a local TV news team did a story on the haunted museum and something interesting showed up on the film. A ghostly woman, said Teri, appeared, looking out of a window of one of the unoccupied houses behind Mordecai House.

Then during the Christmas season when Mordecai House was decked out for the holidays, decorations were mysteriously moved around.

A couple was visiting the upstairs bedroom when the woman felt someone touch her arm. And an employee was alone in the house one day when she heard the sound of frantic footsteps racing from that same bedroom.

Teri was in her office, in a building beside the Mordecai House, when the employee, upset by the occurrence, told her what had happened. "She was almost in tears, shaking and pale," said Teri. "She said she'd been overwhelmed by a horrible sense of sadness and grief and then had heard the fast-paced footsteps upstairs."

Mary?

If so, why did she leave such a strong impression on the mansion—why is it *her* ghost who is seen rather than the others? Mary was born on September 18, 1858. She married William Turk in the parlor of her home. Obviously, her attachment to the place would be strong. Yet we can't say for certain if Mary is responsible for any—or all—of the paranormal activity.

The ghost could also be that of her grandmother, Margaret Lane, who married Moses Mordecai and had three children with him, including Mary's father, Henry. They had all lived in the house together. When Margaret died, Moses married her sister, Ann Lane, and they had a little girl, who Ann named after Margaret.

One has to wonder if she did so out of guilt. Did she, perhaps, feel a little funny about her union with her sister's husband? And what of Mary? Do ghosts feel jealousy and resentment? If so, is that why she sticks around—to claim the house as hers even after the others are long gone?

Sadly for Ann and her baby, Margaret, Moses died before the infant was born.

Perhaps they are *all* there—all of the Mordecai residents living beneath the same roof as one big happy ghostly family. If so, it may get a little crowded.

MORDECAI HOUSE
MORDECAI HISTORIC PARK
1 MIMOSA STREET
RALEIGH, NC 27604
(919) 834-4844

Granger Homestead and Carriage House

Melissa Fox is fascinated by the past. As education director of the Granger Homestead and Carriage House, she shares her enthusiasm with visitors to the historic home–turned–museum and enjoys showing children how to churn butter and make candles. The sense of history is palpable here—especially when the ghosts appear!

In her five years in Canandaigua, at New York's beloved Granger Homestead, she has glimpsed the ghosts twice. "I saw a girl on the porch," she confided, explaining that she was cleaning up after a tea party for a Brownie troop. The young woman in the long white summer dress swished her skirts and walked away as a stunned Melissa watched.

On another occasion, she encountered a different apparition. "I was opening up the house, when I saw the man," said Melissa. She had just opened all of the shutters, and the morning light poured in as she passed the North Parlor. "I was in the hall when I saw him," she said. At first she thought it was a fellow employee, having some fun with her, but then realization hit her. "I did a double take," she said.

Dressed in the fashion of the mid-1800s, the man sat on the couch for a fleeting moment. "It might have been Francis Granger," said Melissa, referring to a one-time resident of the huge home.

About thirty miles southeast of Rochester, New York, the big house was built in 1816 and was home to Gideon Granger, the postmaster general. Four generations of the Granger family made it their home.

Barb Rauscher, who served for two years as social director at the Homestead, also had a startling experience she blames on the Grangers. She still gets goose bumps when she recalls the odd occurrence.

It was about 11 P.M. and she was alone in the enormous house, closing down after an event. She turned off the lights and put things in their proper places, including a cane that had belonged to Francis Granger.

Earlier in the day employees had been discussing a book they'd found about Gideon Granger's political connections in Washington. Barb had made a joke and referred to the possibility of Gideon's "shady dealings."

Apparently, not everyone thought it was funny because she soon found herself on the butt end of an unusual "joke."

Barb set the cane in its place on the table in Francis's room. She was the last one out that night and the first one in the next morning. When she entered Francis's room her gaze fell on the table and a chill shot down her spine.

"The cane was gone," she told me. "I searched the house for days and everyone helped look for it but we could not find it."

The cane had seemingly vanished. Days later, Barb noticed a ray of sunshine spilling through the window. Like a spotlight, it highlighted the linen cupboard in the hall outside of Francis's room. She'd searched just about everywhere else for the valued artifact so she got down on her stomach and peered beneath the cupboard.

Many people have encountered spirits at the Granger Homestead in Canandaigua, New York. (Leslie Rule)

Melissa Fox in the parlor at Granger Homestead where she once saw a man who died over a century ago. (Leslie Rule)

The grounds of the Granger Homestead, where people from the past still linger. (Leslie Rule)

There, glowing in the golden shaft of sunlight, was the cane. "It was a total shock," said Barb. "The hair on the back of my neck stood up."

Spirit encounters are not rare at the Granger Homestead. One museum volunteer told me about the time she was stopped in traffic on the road by the house when she glanced up to see a cluster of women in nineteenth-century black dresses gathered on the veranda. They appeared to be in mourning.

Custodian Dan Eddinger knows every nook and cranny of the lovely old home, and he admits things are a little different there at night than they are in the bright light of day. He learned that firsthand when the alarm system broke down and he was appointed official guardian of the mansion for the night. He settled in on the second-floor couch and tried to doze off but loud banging and phantom footsteps kept him awake. "It was unsettling," he admitted. "I called my wife."

Peggy soon joined him but she was not much comfort. She yawned, took over the couch, and fell into a deep sleep while poor Dan did not get a wink all night.

Who haunts the Granger Homestead?

A doll at the haunted Granger Homestead. (Leslie Rule)

Granger family members? Or perhaps a spirit left over from the days when the family moved out and the house served as a girls' school, where young ladies lived and learned.

Melissa Fox thinks the ghost of the girl in the white dress may have belonged to a past student there.

I wonder if the ghost was Julia.

Julia Ann Williams was the wife of John Albert Granger. The couple's first daughter, Delia Wilson Granger, was welcomed into their family on September 8, 1820.

Sadly, records indicate that Julia was in her early twenties when she died on June 22 two or three years later. She may have died giving birth to her second daughter, also named Julia.

Delia honored her mother by naming one of her daughters Julia—resulting in a line of Julias that was unbroken for at least five generations, including the first Julia.

Today, the estate occupies a lovely ten-acre site, which both the living and the dead can enjoy.

Granger Homestead and Carriage Museum
295 North Main Street
Canandaigua, NY 14424
(585) 394-1472
www.grangerhomestead.org

Island of Ghosts

Nearly seventy miles west of Key West, Florida, the Dry Tortugas seem to float in the turquoise ocean where turtles and sharks and amazingly beautiful fish swim.

Discovered by Ponce de Leon in 1513, the cluster of seven islands drew the attention of the military in the early 1800s. In 1846, the construction of a huge fortress began, yet Fort Jefferson was never finished because new weapon innovations made the military's plans for the fort obsolete.

Famous for its abundant marine life and history of pirates and sunken treasures, the Dry Tortugas is an incredible place for snorkeling.

The Civil War era saw the fort used as a prison, where criminals and army deserters were locked up.

Perhaps the most famous prisoner was Dr. Samuel Mudd, who was accused of conspiring with John Wilkes Booth in the assassination of President Lincoln. After the fort's doctor died of yellow fever, and Mudd took over the medical care there, he received a presidential pardon from Andrew Johnson in 1869.

Today, in addition to being a breathtakingly beautiful place, Fort Jefferson can be spooky—especially at night.

One employee who asked to remain anonymous told me he had spent a couple of weeks there. "It was hard to sleep," he said. "When

The Dry Tortugas are beautiful in the day but can be frighteningly dark at night when the ghosts come out to play. (Leslie Rule)

The ghosts of prisoners may still cling to the place where they were once caged. (Leslie Rule)

there was no moon it was pitch black. I heard what sounded like soldiers marching on asphalt."

He also described an eerie moaning. Rumors of ghosts at Fort Jefferson are whispered about among employees, yet they resist talking to outsiders about the restless spirits there.

Beautiful Birds and a Homely Doll

Audubon House may be caressed by the balmy breezes of Key West, Florida, but visitors shouldn't be surprised if they feel a chill when strolling through the lovely home where naturalist John Audubon once drew tropical birds in the garden.

The 1830 home was built for Captain John Hurling Geiger, who raised his family there. The captain's apparition has been seen in the home, but most of the paranormal activity is focused in the nursery,

A haunted doll mysteriously vanished from the Audubon House in Key West. Did someone steal her or did she run away? (Leslie Rule)

where disembodied voices are heard. It is there that some believe that the ghosts of Geiger children play. While some siblings died of yellow fever in that room, another son was killed when he fell from an almond tree in the yard.

A homely little wax doll with dark circles beneath her eyes and yellow teeth once resided in the museum's nursery. Some say it belonged to a Geiger girl and when she succumbed to yellow fever her spirit inhabited the doll. The doll has been blamed for much of the paranormal activity at Audubon House—including setting off the burglar alarms at night! The doll, however, has mysteriously disappeared.

Stolen?

Or escaped?

Imagine the sickly doll, scurrying along Key West's streets in the moonlight, perhaps leaping out at you when you are least aware.

Or maybe you'd rather not.

AUDUBON HOUSE & TROPICAL GARDENS
295 WHITEHEAD STREET
KEY WEST, FL 33040
(877) 281-BIRD (2473)
WWW.AUDUBONHOUSE.COM

Renovation Vortex

Reports of ghost sightings escalate while old buildings are being remodeled.

Why?

No one, of course, knows the answer to this but many theories are offered. Some say that the commotion and noise "wake up spirits."

Others insist that ghosts residing in a place are upset over the change and appear so that they may protest. (This *does* often result in workmen's hasty retreats!)

Still others cling to the idea that ghosts are grateful that someone is caring for a place that they are fond of, and they make their presence known as a way of showing thanks.

All of these simple explanations may be correct.

A more complex theory embraces the idea that structures trap energy. When the very walls that hold in this energy are altered, the energy is released. The shifting of the physical environment may open a pathway for ghosts to appear.

In some cases, remodeling stops paranormal activity. These incidents support the above-mentioned theory. Perhaps remodeling closes unseen pathways as well as opens them.

Ladder Phenomenon

This writer has noticed an unusually high number of reports of ghost sightings from those on ladders. Is this simply part of the "Renovation Vortex"?

Or is there something about a human putting his or her body at an odd height that creates curiosity in ghosts?

Maybe the act of poking one's head into normally empty space disrupts the energy of a room and opens a door.

More Haunted Museums

Glensheen

This breathtaking mansion-turned-museum could be the pride of Duluth, Minnesota, if it weren't for the skeletons rattling in the closet. Figuratively speaking, that is. The castle-like home was the site of a news-making double murder in June 1977 when mansion heiress eighty-three-year-old Elisabeth Congdon was smothered in her bed. Her nurse, Velma Pietila, was beaten to death with a candlestick.

Prosecutors charged Elisabeth's adopted daughter, Marjorie, and her husband, Roger Caldwell, with the murder, identifying greed as the motive. (Marjorie was in line to inherit a huge chunk of the $8 million estate.) Though Roger was successfully prosecuted, Marjorie was found not guilty. Roger appealed his conviction and ultimately made a deal and was released after spending about five years in prison. (He committed suicide in 1988. Marjorie was later convicted of arson in an unrelated case.)

In July 2003, Minnesota Public Radio reported that the prosecutor in the high-profile case used new DNA technology on an old piece of evidence—an envelope—and confirmed the guilt of Marjorie and Roger.

Ghost enthusiasts insist that the restless spirits of poor Elisabeth and Velma still wander the enormous mansion on the 7.6-acre grounds. Though beautiful, the mansion is so imposing that it was used in scenes of a 1971 thriller starring Patty Duke, called *You'll Like My Mother*.

Roger, who reportedly professed his innocence in his suicide note, may also be roaming the property.

GLENSHEEN
(HISTORIC CONGDON ESTATE)
3300 LONDON ROAD
DULUTH, MN 55804
(888) 454-GLEN (4536)

Pittock Mansion

This 1914 mansion was home to Portland, Oregon, pioneers Henry and Georgiana Pittock, who spent their twilight years enjoying the majestic hilltop view of the city from their grand perch. Henry Pittock's rags-to-riches story began in his teen years when he traveled the Oregon Trail "barefoot and penniless" and went to work for the local paper. Within a decade he was owner and publisher of *The Oregonian,* which is still *the* Portland newspaper.

With its curving marble staircases, high ceilings, and spacious rooms decorated with charming antiques, the Pittock Mansion is a museum enjoyed by many. Yet it has its secrets. Though not widely publicized, paranormal activity has been reported at the Pittock estate. Some say they feel a friendly presence there. One employee confided she had turned off all the lights and locked up for the night only to step

The Pittock Mansion overlooks the Rose City. Do former owners still watch the sunrises from the empty windows? (Leslie Rule)

outside and see *all* of the lights suddenly go back on at once. With the big house's windows blazing, she got in her car and took off.

Do Henry and Georgiana Pittock still roam their dream home? If so, who can blame them?

The sweeping marble staircase at the Pittock Mansion, where unknown ghosts roam. (Leslie Rule)

Meeker Mansion

A friendly presence is believed to haunt the Meeker Mansion in Puyallup, Washington. Built in the valley, with a stunning view of majestic Mount Rainier, the seventeen-room Italianate mansion took three years to build and was completed in 1890 for Ezra and Eliza Jane Meeker when they were close to sixty years old. According to the tour guides of the grand estate, Mrs. Meeker "became smitten with the finer things in life" after a visit to Queen Victoria, so Ezra had the mansion built for his wife.

Ezra Meeker was an extraordinary man who platted and named Puyallup, which translates to "generous people" in the tongue of his northwestern native friends. An author, a successful hop farmer, Puyallup's first mayor, adventurer, and entrepreneur, Ezra lived to be ninety-eight. While his legacy echoes in the sumptuous halls of the Meeker Mansion, it is probably not his ghost that resides there. "He walked away from the house" when his wife died in 1909.

The house became a hospital for a couple of years and later was

What mysterious presence lurks behind the grand walls of the Meeker Mansion in Puyallup, Washington? (Leslie Rule)

bought by a Civil War widows organization, the Ladies of the Grand Army of the Republic. They used it as a retirement home for their members. Then from 1948 to 1970 the house was a nursing home until it was donated to the Meeker Historical Society.

Today it is a museum and available for weddings and special events. Sensitive people insist a pleasant aura surrounds the imposing mansion. Some say a presence lingers on the staircase—a presence so powerful that recent visitors said they could not move past it!

Is it Mr. Meeker or perhaps one of the Ladies of the Grand Army of the Republic who spent their last days there? Or maybe it is something creeping over from next door. Read on for details!

MEEKER MANSION
312 SPRING STREET
PUYALLUP, WA 98372
(253) 848-1770
WWW.MEEKERMANSION.ORG

Haunted Antiques

It is not just *houses* that can become haunted. Sometimes it is the most ordinary of objects. Antiques shops, of course, are filled with everyday objects from days gone by. When an item comes with a past, it may also come with a ghost!

Third Street Antique Mall, which occupies a space smack in front of the Meeker Mansion, is home to some suspicious activity. At one time, the paved parking lot was sweet with the scent of exquisite blossoms, for it was once the site of the Meeker Mansion's rose garden.

Employee Keitha Crain has seen an inexplicable shadow darting through the upstairs several times when she was closing up. "I am a Christian, so I am not afraid," she said, stressing that she does not seek out ghosts or haunted places.

Then there is the mystery of the phantom squirrel, seen by a pair of older shoppers at Third Street Antique Mall. The couple saw the little gray creature scurry over the floor and disappear under a trunk and they hurried to tell management, who immediately investigated. There was, however, no sign of any living critter, leading some to surmise that he was a leftover ghost from the days the area was the Meeker rose garden.

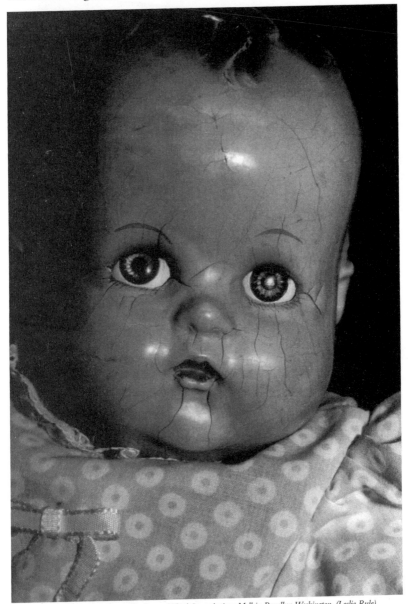

An old doll peers from the shadows of the haunted Third Street Antique Mall in Puyallup, Washington. (Leslie Rule)

The faces of the dead appeared in the mirror of this dresser so often that the frightened owner got rid of it. (Leslie Rule)

Faces in the Mirror

John Cuddeback and his son, Richard, had been in the antiques business in Canandaigua, New York, for over twenty years when they got a strange call in the summer of 2003 from a distraught woman. "Please come get my dresser," she begged. "I don't care what you pay me for it. I just want it out of here."

The old dresser was haunted. The repeated appearance of ghosts in the mirror was disturbing to the woman and she was relieved when the Cuddebacks loaded it into their truck. According to the woman, there had been several deaths in the house, including a suicide.

The dresser was recently purchased, despite the fact the buyer was warned about the unusual feature. No word yet on whether the ghosts are still in the mirror.

Proving the Existence of Ghosts

Do we have concrete evidence that spirits survive past the death of the physical body? Do we have definitive proof that ghosts exist?

No, according to Dr. Sally Rhine Feather, Director of Development at the Rhine Research Center in Durham, North Carolina. In fact, it was this type of evidence that her famous parents, Dr. Joseph Banks Rhine and Dr. Louisa E. Rhine, were seeking when they began their landmark research on psychic ability.

"My folks got into their work via wanting to study the survival question but were stymied because no one had done the basic work on psi [psychic] ability on the living," said Dr. Rhine Feather, coauthor of *The Extraordinary Experiences of Ordinary Americans* (St. Martin's Press, August 2004).

J. B. Rhine coined the term extrasensory perception (ESP) when he authored the book *Extra-Sensory Perception* in 1934. The Rhines' laboratory studies included testing subjects' ability to sense shapes on cards. The cards, which show a star, a plus sign, a circle, wavy lines, and a square were created by the Rhines.

Though Dr. Sally Rhine Feather is still "very, very interested" in the ghost question, she stresses that their existence has not been scientifically proved. As her parents before her did, Dr. Rhine Feather collects stories sent to her by people who say they have seen ghosts.

When it comes to proving the survival of the spirit, Dr. Rhine Feather said, "I think it is the most important question we could ask. Even the most skeptical people stop and listen when they hear you are contemplating research in that area."

Dr. Sally Rhine Feather at the Rhine Research Center in Durham, North Carolina, with a bust of her famous father, Dr. J. B. Rhine, who was known as "the Father of Parapsychology." (Leslie Rule)

Hosts and Ghosts

For about fifty weeks of the year, radio hosts seem to forget I exist. But during the last two weeks of October my schedule is jammed because suddenly they all want to talk about ghosts! One Halloween season I was interviewed seventy times in the ten days leading up to the spooky holiday.

Most of the hosts do not have time to read the copies of my book that my publisher sends them but ask polite questions. And some want to talk to me just for laughs and ask me inane questions about Scooby-Doo, the cartoon canine who travels with a paranormal investigative team. Though many of these interviews take place at 4 A.M., about six hours before my normal wake-up time, that is okay with me, as I don't have to get out of my pajamas! The beauty of radio is that a guest can be interviewed over the phone.

A surprisingly high percentage of radio hosts put me on hold after the interviews and as soon as there is a commercial break they privately share a personal ghost story. It wasn't long before I realized that these stories belong in their very own chapter.

Here are a few of the fascinating accounts that radio personalities have shared with me:

A Summer Chill

Morning-show host Eddie Fingers
The Dawn Patrol
WEBN Radio
Cincinnati, Ohio

It was a summer night in 2002, when Eddie Fingers and his wife, Debbie, stayed up late watching television. When Eddie dozed off around 2 A.M., Debbie turned off the TV and went upstairs to bed while her husband slept on the couch.

"I woke up a short time later, disoriented from my nap," said Eddie, explaining that he noted the TV was off and he started to look away when "reflected movement in the screen caught my attention. I started to turn around to see what it was but as I did, the reflected movement passed from left to right on my screen."

Stunned, Eddie watched as a woman and a boy in nineteenth-century dress crossed the screen. "The image was quite plain," Eddie said, describing the bonnet and the long brownish dress with the bustle the woman wore. The boy wore short pants and a small bow tie. "I wasn't able to make out facial features due to the low light reflection. They moved slowly and silently. I sat stunned and—yes, scared stiff—for a couple of seconds, afraid to turn around. Then I thought, *Jeez, what's wrong with me?*"

For a moment, he tried to reason with himself. Surely it must have been his wife and son he'd seen. "I turned around *hoping* to see them. There was nothing there!"

Eddie froze, pondering the idea he had just seen a pair of ghosts. His Cincinnati area property backs up to many acres of untouched forestland. The figures had appeared to be in the kitchen, just inside the sliding glass door that opened into the wilderness beyond.

"Many goose bumps later, I did what any man would do. I ran upstairs and hid under the covers with my wife."

Thelma's Tricks

Erskine

Erskine Overnight (syndicated)

Erskine, the host of a nationally syndicated radio program that often probes paranormal topics has had more than his share of surreal experiences.

"I lived in a haunted house about fifteen years ago," said the host of the edgy weekend show, adding that he and his wife, Charlotte, nicknamed the place "Haunted Hollow" because of all the strange things that happened there.

The Borden, Indiana, two-story house was a little isolated and sat on a wooded ten-acre lot. "Our nearest neighbors were a herd of cows," he said. "The house was about 150 years old and there had been some strange deaths there."

Once the site of a bootleg business, some believed that the homestead was haunted by the ghosts of a couple of moonshiners who were murdered there. "One person was killed with a corn knife in the middle of my driveway," Erskine told me, explaining that the weapon resembled a large machete.

But the unexplained phenomena that surrounded the home had a mischievous quality to it and Erskine and Charlotte came to suspect the ghost belonged to a child. That theory was strengthened when they and their guests began to see a small shadowy shape darting through the house. The apparition was child-sized and the mischief smacked of a naughty little boy.

"One morning we got up and found dog food in the oven," said Erskine. Someone or *something* had dumped fifty pounds of dog food into the oven.

Another time the couple was startled when their Siamese cat, Sam, appeared to be dragged across the room by an invisible presence. It was as if someone had him by the tail, and the cat clawed at the rug, trying to pull himself forward as he skidded backward.

The other cat, Spazmo, a big orange tabby, watched with wide startled eyes. "He ran to the utility room and got on top of the water heater and didn't leave that room for five years," said Erskine.

They were surprised when they learned that the naughty little ghost was not a boy, but a girl. A visitor to the home told them that one of her relatives had once lived in the house—a little girl named Thelma, who died of dysentery. "She told us that Thelma was a tomboy," said Erskine.

Thelma also seemed to enjoy giving gifts. "She left pennies all over the house," said Erskine. Most inexplicable was the 1991 penny they found—in 1990! "We took it to the bank and showed it to them. They said it was counterfeit."

That, of course, did not make sense. Why would someone counterfeit pennies with future dates? But it was the only explanation that would make sense to the bankers.

Charlotte had a favorite necklace and for years she'd shopped for the perfect pair of earrings to match it to no avail. One morning, she woke up on her birthday to find that a pair of earrings had mysteriously materialized in the middle of the kitchen table. "They matched the necklace perfectly," said Erskine, who could only conclude they were a gift from a friendly little ghost.

While Erskine and Charlotte were rarely pestered by the ghost, they had a house sitter who felt differently. They returned from a trip to find her sitting on top of her suitcase in the middle of the kitchen floor.

"She looked at us and didn't even say hello," said Erskine. "She told us, 'It didn't bother me when the canisters moved around. It didn't bother me when I saw weird lights in the house. But it *did* bother me when I packed my suitcase and woke up to find my clothes strewn all over the house with my bras going around on the ceiling fan.'"

It may be difficult to keep a house sitter when you live in a haunted house, but Erskine mentions one big plus. "When you have ghosts around, you never get broken into."

Still Cooking

Diana Jordan

This busy TV/radio personality is featured on the following: host of *Between the Lines* (AP Radio Network), and Morning News anchor of

K-Lite 106.7 FM of Portland, Oregon. Diana is also the book reviewer for the popular Portland morning show *AM Northwest* on KATU-TV.

Two decades have passed since Diana Jordan first saw the "perfect white house with pillars." "It was in a dream," she confided. The very next day as she took a drive through Portland, Oregon, she turned onto a street she was unfamiliar with—S.E. Holgate. She was astonished to see the house in her dream. "There was a For Rent sign on the lawn."

Radio host Diana Jordan once met a friendly ghost in her kitchen. (Courtesy of Diana Jordan)

Before long, she had moved into the two-story house with the full basement. "As a journalist, I've covered all kinds of stories," said Diana, who is usually very brave. "But I discovered once we moved in that I was afraid to go upstairs."

Something about the top floor gave her the creeps. "It was as if it were haunted," she confided. Though she rarely ventured upstairs, she did meet a ghost.

Diana got out of bed one morning and as she padded barefoot into the kitchen, she smelled bacon cooking. There, in the middle of the kitchen, was an older woman who smiled kindly at her. "Good morning, dear," the woman chirped. "Would you like breakfast?"

The sound of bacon crackling filled the air as she stared at the woman. "She was grandmotherly with short, softly curled white hair," said Diana. "She was wearing an apron. It was white and trimmed in cobalt blue and there were little flowers all over it. It had two big pockets that matched the fabric."

The image was so vivid that all these years later, she can still close her eyes and picture it.

"It was as if she belonged there," remembered Diana. "It was as if I were a guest in her house and it was her natural inclination to feed me breakfast."

As the smiling woman waited for a response, Diana found herself politely replying, "No, thank you."

"It seemed like the most natural scene in the world—until I remembered that I didn't know this woman," explained Diana. "It seemed like I knew her and that it was *her* kitchen in *her* house. I had no fear, despite the fact that I was wary of other parts of the house. When the scene vanished, I felt delighted that I had glimpsed a ghost."

The next time Diana saw her landlord she told him about the odd occurrence.

"Oh," he said nonchalantly. "That was just my mom. She lived there until she died."

More Hosts and Ghosts

The John Peterson Show
WIBA Radio
Middleton, Wisconsin

John remembers visiting family friends in an old farmhouse when he was just a boy. He wandered into a cluttered room and as he crawled along the floor he came upon a pair of very old shoes. As his eyes traveled upward he saw *someone* was wearing them! He screamed at the sight of the ghost of an elderly man. Everyone came running. When he told the grown-ups what he'd seen, the hostess said he had just met the ghost of her dead husband.

Wendy Riddle
The Morning Show
WFNC Radio
Fayetteville, North Carolina

Host Wendy Riddle will never forget her creepy encounter with the spirit world! She was a tiny girl, sleeping in a crib by her parents' bed. In the middle of the night she called out to her mother, complaining she was too warm. Her mother advised her to stick her legs out of the crib to cool off. She did so. Then she heard the sound of little footsteps running across the room toward her. The unknown entity slapped her on the leg!

These days, Wendy keeps all her limbs in the bed when she's sleeping.

On the Mark
KNWZ AM Radio
Palm Desert, California

Norman Mark was heartbroken when his best friend had a fatal heart attack as the two swam laps in a public pool. He was guilt ridden, sure that he had pushed his friend too hard—until his friend's spirit appeared to him at home. The apparition smiled and shook his head as if to reassure him. Three years later he learned from his friend's widow that she had also seen the man's spirit around the same time.

JLB
The Morning Show
WICC Radio
Bridgeport, Connecticut

JLB and two others saw an apparition while doing the news. It appeared as a three-dimensional light that glided past them.

"Did you keep your composure?" this writer asked.

"No!" JLB replied. "We told everyone what was happening!"

They have never figured out the source of the very unusual breaking news.

Haunted Hotels

The Worthington Inn

It is strange to imagine Ohio as the Wild West. Yet at one time, the city of Worthington, Ohio, crouched at the edge of the western wilderness.

Glowing eyes peered from the darkness beyond. And when it was night it was indeed dark—the kind of inky darkness that only hundreds of miles of untamed land can produce. In the early 1800s when Worthington land was settled, western states such as Idaho, Washington, and Oregon did not exist and were nothing but forested, untouched terrain.

It was 1816 and Rensselaer W. Cowles was just twenty when he traveled from his home in Connecticut to settle in Worthington. Two years later he married twenty-one-year-old Laura Kilbourne. She was the daughter of original Worthington settler Reverend James Kilbourne. R.W. purchased three lots for a grand total of $250 and in 1834 built a mansion for his family.

Today that mansion still stands. It is the Worthington Inn, an exquisitely charming inn with twenty-six opulently decorated rooms, and an award-winning restaurant and pub. In the heart of Worthington's Historic District, the inn looks upon a clean wide street lined with enormous shade trees.

The staff has a policy of treating guests "like family." While that warmth made my stay enjoyable, it was something else that made it *memorable*.

It was at the Worthington Inn that I had one of my rare encounters with a ghost. While researching, I visit countless haunted places but I do not expect to experience the paranormal. I simply interview others about their encounters and examine the history of a place.

I spent three nights at the Worthington Inn. It was a hot Sunday afternoon when I awoke from a nap and decided to take a stroll. Two hours earlier, the restaurant and pub had been brimming with hungry people having brunch. As I walked down the carpeted hall past the pub, I heard a woman laugh. I figured brunch was still in full swing.

I continued on, planning to exit through the lobby, when two steps later, I changed my mind and backtracked to exit through the pub. I stepped into the bar and my mouth fell open. The place was empty. The silence overwhelmed me.

Just seconds before, someone in there had laughed.

Who?

I rushed through the bar and into the restaurant, searching for the laughing lady. I even peeked into the kitchen. There was no one there.

Had I heard a *ghost*?

Though ghost encounters are unusual for me, they certainly aren't unusual at the Worthington Inn. Night auditor Kandice Robertson-Fuentes was taking a break and sitting in the empty bar when she was startled to see a man in the mirror. He wore a black suit and a bowler hat. Kandice quickly glanced behind her, but there was no one there. She looked back at the mirror and he was still reflected there. As she watched, "he walked steadily to the end of the bar," she said, explaining that he was visible until he reached the edge of the mirror. "At the same time there was a strong scent of cigar smoke."

Banquet manager Frank Cody was upstairs late one night, and as he was turning off the lights he saw a man walk into a darkened room. Curious, he followed the man and flicked on the light. "There was no one in there," he said, shaking his head.

On another day, an employee had just finished setting up the tables for a banquet when his supervisor scolded him for not getting the job done. He turned to see that someone—or *something*—had just undone his work, scooting the silverware, napkins, and glasses to the edges of the tables.

Who are the ghosts who inhabit the Worthington Inn?

They may be the very first inhabitants of the huge home—the Cowles family. R. W. and Laura moved into the mansion in 1834. While R. W. made a name for himself, Laura made babies. R. W., a successful merchant, also served as county commissioner, justice of the peace, and postmaster.

Records show that ten children were born to the couple. Yet six of those died in childhood. A boy toddler died on August 12, 1828, of dysentery. Another heartbreaking August, in 1832, saw the deaths of one-month-old baby Laura and James Whitfield Cowles, her five-year-old brother. The first day of spring 1834 took toddler Rensselaer away with scarlet fever.

Dysentery again plucked a child from his mother's arms in September 1835, when three-year-old Granville succumbed.

Apparently Granville was a special family name, for two boys received it while both were still alive. The second Granville, born on August 18, 1833, lived to be fifty-two.

In 1840, death again reached out its greedy fingers and snatched five-year-old Gertrude.

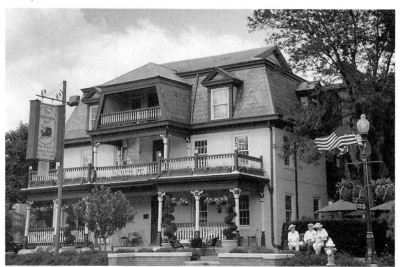

The past has never left the old Worthington Inn in Worthington, Ohio. (Leslie Rule)

It is mind boggling to imagine life for Laura. The young woman spent over a decade giving birth and burying babies. How did she go on? Did she get down on her knees and thank God for the four who made it to adulthood?

Life was different then. In these days of cell phones and computers it is hard to wrap the mind around a world without running water, electricity, and cars.

Our ancestors lived tough lives. Families saw many members die young. But did a broken heart hurt any less?

We see a pattern in haunted places. Often they are the sites of extremely emotional scenes. The Cowles family certainly had their share of emotion.

But the history of the house did not end with the Cowles.

In 1852, ten years after R.W. died at age forty-six, Theodore Fuller purchased the home, enlarged it, and turned it into a tavern called Central House. It changed hands again and was operated as a hotel with livery stables that offered stagecoaches for hire. Columbus residents traveled there for oyster suppers and dancing in the third-floor ballroom. An old hotel register shows that "Harvey Firestone and party, Detroit, Michigan" stayed there on December 28, 1891.

At the turn of the century a fire destroyed the roof and damaged the hotel's top floor. Time marched on and the property changed hands several times. It's been known as the Bishop House, Union Hotel, Central House, and New England Inn.

In the early 1950s, the WRFD radio station occupied the top floors of the building. By the 1980s, the big old house was in sorry shape and in danger of demolition, when it was rescued by a $3 million restoration.

When the building was saved, the ghosts of the past were rescued too.

THE WORTHINGTON INN
649 HIGH STREET
WORTHINGTON, OH 43085
(614) 885-2600
WWW.WORTHINGTONINN.COM

More Haunted Hotels

The Gulfstream Hotel

Built in 1924, the Gulfstream Hotel is a nine-story pink hotel near the beach in Lake Worth, Florida. As a historic landmark and a member of Historic Hotels of America, it naturally has at least one ghost. According to the hotel staff, TVs turn themselves on, phantom prank phone calls are made from within the hotel, and an unseen presence taps people on their shoulders and tugs on their sleeves. The ghost, they believe, also plays games with the elevator.

It is the elevator that may be the source of the haunting. According to the hotel staff, it was the scene of a tragedy in the 1930s when a little girl fell down the elevator shaft. The child died and it is her mischievous spirit that is credited with haunting the hotel!

THE GULFSTREAM HOTEL
1 LAKE AVENUE
LAKE WORTH, FL 33460
(888) 540-0669
(561) 540-6000
WWW.THEGULFSTREAMHOTEL.COM

The Stanley Hotel

The Stanley Hotel, tucked into the foothills of the Rocky Mountains, is listed in the National Register of Historic Places. This Georgian Colonial Revival–styled hotel has another claim to fame. It is said to be the inspiration for horror writer Stephen King's *The Shining*. Hotel staff report that King was staying there when he witnessed the ghost of a little boy wandering in the hotel corridor on the second floor.

With 138 guest rooms, the hotel was recently restored to its "former grandeur" and features views of the Rocky Mountains, and a sumptuous Sunday brunch, as well as a place on the paranormal map.

Guests confide they've heard invisible children playing in the hallways and seen objects move about on their own. Some say they've spotted a ghostly little girl crying in a corner.

Hotel bartenders report the appearance of Freelan Oscar Stanley, the original hotel owner (also of Stanley Steam Car fame). They say that his apparition wears a black jacket and a top hat. He is seen passing the bar and then vanishes before startled observers' eyes.

Freelan was dying from tuberculosis when he moved to the area and built the hotel in the early 1900s. Yet he lived several more decades, dying at age ninety-one.

Many folks say they've spotted the spirit of Freelan's wife, Flora, throughout the hotel—usually on the staircase. Though she died as an elderly lady, her ghost manifests as a middle-aged version. Flora's Steinway piano remains on the site and when it mysteriously plays on its own the music is credited to her phantom fingers dancing over the keys.

THE STANLEY HOTEL

333 WONDERVIEW AVENUE

ESTES PARK, CO 80517

(800) 976-1377

WWW.STANLEY HOTEL.COM

The Jefferson Hotel

This historic hotel in Jefferson, Texas, is over 150 years old and is believed to be home to numerous ghosts. The mischief-making spirits are credited with turning on water faucets, slamming doors, and playing with the light switches. Doris Hoosier, a front-desk clerk at the hotel, has grown accustomed to the naughty ghosts' antics. "We had some ladies staying here and they went on the local ghost tour," she remembered. "When they got back, they went to their room and suddenly came screaming down the hall. When I asked them what had happened they said that someone had switched their luggage."

Doris listened as they explained that all of the clothes had been removed from the suitcases and switched to the opposite suitcases. She suggested that one of their friends was playing a trick on them but they insisted that everyone had left for the tour at the same time and they were the first to return.

Doris also recalled an incident when a guest returned to her room to find herself locked out by the chain lock—an inexplicable occurrence, as there was no one in the room.

Located in the historic Riverfront District, this building has played many roles. It once was used as a warehouse to store cotton. In the 1920s, it was a hotel called the Crystal Palace, where visitors danced to ragtime music.

No one has pinpointed which era created the spirits that roam the hotel. Guests have seen the ghosts of a blonde woman and a man in a long coat. They have also heard the sad crying of a phantom child.

THE JEFFERSON HOTEL

124 WEST AUSTIN STREET

JEFFERSON, TX 75657

(903) 665-2631

WWW.HISTORICJEFFERSONHOTEL.COM

Mendocino Hotel & Garden Suites

The lady waits patiently, her hands folded neatly in her lap. She sits in a chair by the window, staring intently outside. Her dress is elegant and old-fashioned, her long skirts flowing primly past her ankles.

Poof. She is gone.

She is the sweet spirit of the Mendocino Hotel. The 1878 artifact of Mendocino, California, stands looking out at the mouth of the Big River and the endless Pacific Ocean beyond. This classy historic hotel is adorned with antiques—antiques that likely make people from the past feel right at home.

In addition to appearing in the chair beside the window, the lady ghost is said to materialize in the restaurant and especially in the mirrors there. In fact, diners frequently "ask for the haunted table," according to front-desk clerk Andi Fry, who has had her share of odd occurrences at the hotel. She recalled the night that a couple left their room through the French doors and stepped out onto the balcony. When they tried to return, the door had been bolted from the inside—impossible in an empty room. "That same night everything went wrong," she remembered. "My adding machine came up with numbers that I hadn't punched in and the phones kept going dead." Stranger still was the fact that fifty extra dollars appeared in the safe at the same time fifty dollars came up missing from the till. "I know I didn't move the money," she insisted. It seems the ghost made a deposit for her!

Who is the ghost that haunts the Mendocino? Legend has it that she is the wife of a fisherman waiting for him to return from the sea.

This writer, however, wonders if she might be Mary Bever, who was born Mary Hogan in Ireland in 1846. At twenty she married Benjamin Bever and together they ran the hotel (once known as the Central Hotel). It is said that many were fond of her, as she was such a fine hostess and nurturing spirit dying childless at seventy.

Though the apparition seen at the Mendocino Hotel is that of a younger woman, it is possible that she manifests as she appeared at a happy time in her life.

MENDOCINO HOTEL & GARDEN SUITES
45080 MAIN STREET
MENDOCINO, CA 95460
(707) 937-0511
(800) 548-0513
WWW.MENDOCINOHOTEL.COM

A Haunting with a *Smile*

John Saldana was busy at the front desk of the Emily Morgan Hotel in San Antonio, Texas, when an attractive young woman in a red dress entered the lobby. "She was very pretty with blonde hair," he said. The woman smiled at him as she crossed the lobby and passed behind a column. He watched, expecting her to emerge from the other side but a long moment passed and there was no sign of her. "I jumped over the counter because I couldn't believe what I'd seen," he said. He looked behind the column, but she had vanished.

Night auditor at the hotel a stone's throw from the Alamo, John has had ten years to experience the ghosts at the historic structure, which was the Medical Arts Building for five decades. Built in 1928, the towering

At one time the Emily Morgan Hotel was the Medical Arts Building. Do the ghosts of past patients haunt the upper floors? (Leslie Rule)

The ghost of a pretty woman in a red dress has been seen in the lobby of the Emily Morgan Hotel in San Antonio, Texas.
(Leslie Rule)

building's upper floors were used as the hospital while the lower ones served as doctors' and dentists' offices. Guests who stay on the fourteenth floor sometimes call the front desk in the middle of the night to complain about the sounds of noisy carts rattling by their doors. "The floor is carpeted," John said, pointing out that the sounds they hear may actually be echoing from a time long past—when nurses pushed gurneys and carts of medicine over the linoleum floor.

"I've had only a few experiences," said John, who once saw the shadowy figure of a man in a blue uniform in the hotel's restaurant's kitchen. "The hair on the back of my neck stood up," he said. At the time it was the middle of the night and just he and a female security guard were at work in the hotel. When John shared his encounter with her she nodded knowingly, for she, too, had once seen the ghost of a man in a blue uniform in the kitchen. The apparition had smiled at him and then turned away. She followed him, not suspecting he was an ethereal being, until he melted into the air.

Sometimes the clanking of pots and pans is heard in the empty kitchen and phone calls to the front desk originate from unoccupied offices. John finds this chilling but not as strange as an encounter that has him still shaking his head. "It was four in the morning," he said, explaining he was busy with paperwork, when he looked up to see an older man in full Catholic-priest attire.

"Hi. How can I help you?" asked John.

"Is this hotel haunted?" asked the priest.

Sensitive about not alarming guests, John cautiously asked, "Why do you ask?"

"I was woken up by someone at my door," said the man. "I looked out the peephole and didn't see anyone. So I opened the door and looked into the hallway. I saw an old woman floating in the hall."

"Maybe she appeared to you because she knows you are strong-hearted," said John, expressing his belief that ghosts never appear to people with weak hearts. "Maybe she had a message for you."

The elderly priest smiled and walked away. As he got on the elevator John went back to his paperwork, but an instant later he looked up and noticed something odd. "The elevator wasn't moving," he said.

The priest did not emerge, and the elevator remained at the lobby level. John later asked his coworkers if they knew of a priest staying at the hotel, but they had not seen the man, nor did a priest check out in the following days. Perhaps he had simply changed to street clothes, but John still finds the encounter puzzling.

"I've thought about it a lot," he said. "Why did he get dressed in his full priest attire at four in the morning?"

And why didn't the elevator move?

Was the mysterious priest a ghost?

It is interesting to note that that most of the encounters John described ended with the ghost smiling. ·

EMILY MORGAN HOTEL
705 EAST HOUSTON STREET
SAN ANTONIO, TX 78205
(210) 225-5100
(800) 784-1180
WWW.EMILYMORGANHOTEL.COM

The Blennerhassett Hotel

The Blennerhassett Hotel, a five-story brick building with two towered corners, is just across the Ohio border beside the Ohio River, in Parkersburg, West Virginia. The hotel has gone through many incarnations since its grand opening in 1889. It has been a bank, a drugstore, and a series of nightclubs.

Employees and guests have had countless ghost sightings, including that of the apparition of a little boy who appears in the lobby. The child wears vintage clothing and holds a newspaper.

One former employee, who apparently had the ability to see ghosts more easily than others, once informed the night auditor, Alaina Cline, that he often saw the ghost of a little girl following her. Though Alaina could not see the spirit, she admitted, "I feel like there is a presence near me."

Sometimes when the hotel is quiet and the air is still, a sudden gust will whoosh past Alaina as if an invisible friend has been trotting along beside her. Alaina noted other odd things such as the inexplicable scent of cigar smoke in the empty bar, the blurry faces reflected in the tile floor when no other people are around, and the phantom knocking on her office door.

She shivered, recalling the quiet night she was alone in her office and heard a rap on the door. Thinking that the security guard or the janitor had forgotten their keys, she opened the door. No one was there. Five minutes later she again heard the knocking.

"I figured someone was playing a trick on me," said Alaina. She tried to ignore the rapping but it grew louder, so again she opened the door. "I stood there a minute, feeling a little bit freaked out," she said. At that moment she glanced up to see the janitor and a security guard coming down the stairs. "There was no way it could have been them."

Who haunts the Blennerhassett?

According to author Susan Sheppard, founder of the Haunted Parkersburg Ghost Tours, the ghost of William N. Chancellor resides at the historic hotel. He grew up in the city, built the hotel, and spent two terms as the city's mayor.

The Blennerhassett Hotel, in Parkersburg, West Virginia, is brimming with ghosts. (Leslie Rule)

"After the hotel reopened in 1986, guests reported waking up to see a distinguished older gentleman," explained Susan. "He stood at the foot of their beds in a three-piece gray suit. He would stare at them with a melancholy expression, but fade quickly, leaving a lingering scent of pipe or cigar smoke."

How could she be sure the ghost was that of William Chancellor?

His portrait, she pointed out, hangs in the hotel's library. "Many who saw the portrait say he is the man they saw beside their beds."

The apparition has also been seen strolling throughout the hotel, most frequently in the oldest sections. And one night he seemed ready to take Susan's ghost tour!

It was a crisp fall evening when tour guide Doni Enoch spotted an old man headed for the library, where visitors gathered before the tour. "She was concerned because she thought the fellow might be too elderly to make the two-mile walk," said Susan.

Doni followed the man to the library and when she stepped into the room was astonished to find it empty. "Just as she realized she may have seen Mr. Chancellor's spirit, something strange happened," Susan continued. "She glanced down and saw the keys of the antique typewriter move. They typed the letters 'J' and 'K.'"

Doni blinked, wondering if she was seeing things. Then she noticed a photograph on the table. It was a picture of John F. Kennedy, who visited Parkersburg in 1960.

It is likely that the ghost many spot is indeed William Chancellor. Who are the others?

Records show that William had a young son who died before the hotel was built. William Nelson Chancellor, Jr., died on June 1, 1875, at not quite three years of age. Could he have followed his father to the hotel? Is he one of the mischievous spirits?

Of course they could also be the ghosts of past guests. Or perhaps they are customers or employees who spent time there when the building was a bank or a drugstore.

"The hotel is located near a Civil War hospital, where ghosts of Union soldiers, trapped in a twilight world, are believed to roam," said Susan.

Perhaps some of the ghosts have wandered over from the old hospital. Whoever they are, there seems to be more than a few. Just ask anyone who has spent a restless night in one of the more haunted rooms there. It is common for guests to report rowdy parties with shouting and blaring music. When employees follow up on the complaints and check out the supposed party they always find an unoccupied room.

THE BLENNERHASSETT HOTEL
320 MARKET STREET
PARKERSBURG, WV 26101
(304) 422-3131
(800) 262-2536
WWW.THEBLENNERHASSETT.COM

Cemetery Stories

Why in the world would a soul stay close to an empty body? The flesh, after all, is *just* flesh. In this writer's opinion, our bodies without souls are about as meaningful as cantaloupe rinds rotting on the garbage heap.

When nature takes its course, the earth swallows us whole. Time turns our bones to dust and our spirits are free to go to places the imagination can't even comprehend. Haunted cemeteries make no sense to me. Logic says that souls freed from bodies would not be obligated to stay tethered to those bodies.

But what do *I* know? Authoring a ghost book does not make me an expert on the afterlife and the intentions of ghosts. I know only what witnesses tell me. And witness after witness has come forward with compelling accounts of spirits who linger near places where their bodies are laid to rest.

Here are some examples:

French Quarter Nightmare

When Linda Malone was a little girl, her Irish grandmother regaled her with stories of ghosts and leprechauns and other strange creatures from "the other side." She always figured that one day she would meet a ghost. "I just never suspected that it would happen on a lovely spring day at high noon," she said.

It was in 1989 when Linda and her now ex-husband traveled from Seattle to New Orleans. They stayed in the French Quarter the week after Mardi Gras. The city, famous for its wild party, had quieted and Linda was excited about seeing the sights—especially the old St. Louis Cemetery Number One, where Marie Laveau, voodoo queen, was laid to rest.

Linda's husband grumbled impatiently as the two took a cab to the graveyard. "The only thing on *his* mind was touring the Superdome," explained Linda.

They were dropped off at the gate of the cemetery. "You can see the Superdome from the entrance to the cemetery," said Linda. "My husband looked longingly in its direction and then informed me that there was no one to tell us how to find Marie's grave and that we might as well just go to the Dome."

"There *has* to be a groundskeeper," Linda retorted. "I'm not leaving until I see the voodoo queen's tomb!"

The couple entered the cemetery and began wandering aimlessly over the rolling terrain. The grass was green and mowed, but most of the old tombs were deteriorating under the weight of the years.

As they rounded a curve, they spotted an elderly black man sitting atop a crumbling tomb. "At first I thought he was asleep," Linda remembered. "He was just sitting there with his hands in his lap and his head down. He had very dark skin and some gray in his short cropped hair."

His old-fashioned clothing struck Linda as odd. His black shoes were square-toed and his shirt had no collar.

Linda nudged her husband. "Go see if he is awake. Ask him if he knows where Marie's tomb is."

But when he approached the old man and spoke to him, there was no response.

"I actually wondered if he might be dead," said Linda. Of course, that made no sense, as the man sat upright. After a moment the stranger stirred.

"The old man slowly rose and paused a moment with his square black hands at his side and his head still down. He never looked up. He shuffled around to face one of the little pathways and started off at a very slow pace."

They followed him and Linda was surprised to hear him speak. "The old woman, the old witch," he mumbled. "They all come to see the old woman."

"The path went over a knoll and then another," said Linda. "We lost sight of the entrance and we didn't see any other people. The old gentleman just kept moving and mumbling."

Suddenly they were upon the grave. It was heaped with flowers, coins, bottles of wine, and Mardi Gras beads—offerings from others who had come to pay their respects. "I pulled out my camera and whispered to my husband that he should give the old man some money. He reached for his wallet as I snapped a picture, and then I heard him say, 'Where is he?'"

The old man had vanished.

"I literally turned in place, but he was nowhere to be seen," said Linda. "The hair on the back of my neck went straight up. The sun was warm and there was not a cloud in the sky, but I had a chill. The old man was gone. There was nowhere for him to hide. The tombs were broken down. He was slow as a turtle. How could he move fast enough to hide and why would he *want* to?"

Linda watched as her nearly hysterical husband raced around the area, searching for the old man. Finally he grabbed Linda's arm and said, "We are leaving! *Now!*"

"My husband toured the Superdome, the marriage ended, and life went on," said Linda. "I have never been back to New Orleans. The old gentleman has stayed in my mind. Was he a ghost, a familiar, or one of the undead? Was he put there to make sure that those who wanted to honor the old queen would be allowed to do so? Or was he there only to scare my husband half to death?"

Linda smiled and added, "My husband drank more than usual at dinner that night and for several nights after."

Amidst the Dead

When Nancy Fischer was researching her roots at a New York historical society, she was drawn to an old map she found in the archives.

"I'd never heard of Old Williamsburg before," said the mother of a grown daughter, explaining that she soon learned the forgotten town is situated in western New York, between Geneseo and Mount Morris.

Settled in the 1700s, the town was devastated by disease, which killed most of the population. Though Old Williamsburg was abandoned in 1807, the gravestones of those who once lived there remain, nestled in farmland, the grass around them neatly trimmed by the cattle who graze there.

"I knew that a lot of my family was from that area and thought I might find an ancestor there," said Nancy. It was a brilliant August afternoon when she hopped in her car and drove the thirty miles from her home in Canandaigua in search of Old Williamsburg.

She knew she had found it when she saw an old headstone. "It was peeking out from the trees," she said. She pulled over and parked her car. She was immediately struck by the silence. It was so quiet, not even a bee buzzed.

She glanced toward the trees and at the gravestone beyond. It glinted in the sunlight and she headed toward it, wading through tall grass as brier bushes reached out thorny branches and caught at her pant legs.

A moment later she was *there*.

"It was a beautiful, peaceful graveyard," said Nancy. Sunshine fell through the branches of the trees, speckling the green grass with golden light. She gazed up in awe at the maple, poplar, and beechnut trees—trees so huge she knew they must have been there for centuries.

Hundreds of gravestones surrounded her and she pulled out her notebook and began to record names and dates. "I figured that even if I didn't find any relatives, that the historical society would like to have the information."

As Nancy worked, she found herself enjoying the tranquillity. "It was the most peaceful place I've ever been. It was so quiet, with no sound of traffic."

She was recording a name from about the fiftieth stone, when someone spoke.

"Nancy."

Though she didn't recognize the friendly male voice, she smiled and turned around. "I thought someone had seen my car and was playing a trick on me."

"Okay!" Nancy called out. "Who is there?" She waited expectantly, the smile still pasted on her face, but no one emerged from the trees.

"Okay, the game is on," said Nancy. It *had* to be someone who knew her. "I wasn't scared. I got back to work, but kept looking behind me."

As she continued to record names, she heard it again. *"Nancy!"* This time it was said with more urgency.

"I turned around and watched the trees for a long time, my eyes flitting from one to another, looking for an elbow or a person peeking out."

"All right," she said. "Somebody's messing around here!" She started walking toward the trees where the voice had come from. "The silence was penetrating," she confided. "The hair on the back of my neck started to rise. I was beginning to feel a little afraid."

Uneasy now, she dropped the idea of searching for the prankster and turned back to her work. As soon as she began writing, he spoke again—this time sounding as if he were right behind her.

"Nancy, why are you searching for the living amidst the dead?"

She whirled around but no one was there. Yet the voice had been so loud and clear. Frightened, she ran to her car. Her hands were shaking but she managed to unlock the door, scramble in, and start the engine.

"The words sounded so familiar. I knew I had heard them somewhere before. When I got home I called a friend who is a Bible scholar. She said, 'Oh, yes. That's from Luke, chapter twenty-four, verse five. That's what was spoken by two men in dazzling apparel who appeared to the two Marys as they discovered Jesus' tomb empty.'"

Nancy admits that the event shook her up so much that it "put a sharp end to my genealogy search for a while. I wondered if I should be paying more attention to things in the living world."

Was the disembodied voice one of a helpful spirit delivering an important message to Nancy? *Or,* perhaps, did it belong to a ghost who was just having a little fun?

Though she can't say for sure, Nancy is certain of one thing. She will never forget it!

Traffic Stop

Caroline and Candy Steinken are sisters-in-law and best friends. The two Wisconsin women who married brothers often share secrets but they never imagined that one day they would share a secret so strange that they simply could not keep it.

Both moms needed a break from caring for their families the freezing January evening they bundled up and drove to the Chicago suburbs to see a movie. "It was a comedy," said Candy, describing how they were laughing afterward as Caroline steered her Dodge onto a well-lit street.

Caroline saw him first. Off to her left, striding across the lawn of one of the old, charming houses that lined the street, was a man. Something about him was not right. *He is not dressed warm enough for such a cold night,* she thought as he headed toward them. "He wore jeans and a flannel shirt with a vest," she said.

"The wind chill was forty below," added Candy. "It was a record-setting cold day."

Moving at a brisk pace, the man stepped into the road right into the path of an oncoming car. "The car slammed on its brakes at the same time we did," said Caroline.

Candy watched the man and described his clothing just as Caroline did, adding a few details. "He was wearing a flannel shirt, like a farmer, a pair of jeans, and work boots." Besides the fact he was not dressed for such a cold night, there was something even more odd about him. He was *transparent.* "You could see the headlights from the other cars shining through him," Caroline explained.

He passed by one headlight of the other car and just as he moved in front of the other headlight he vanished. "He swirled into a haze and dissipated," said Candy.

I couldn't have seen that! thought Caroline. "I had my mouth open," she remembered. "And I looked at Candy and she had her mouth open too."

Candy admitted, "I would have been glad to call it a hallucination but as Caroline and I looked at each other with our mouths hanging open, we instantly went into shock. We knew by looking at each other that what we'd seen was real."

Both cars sat still for a very long moment. It was obvious that the driver of the other car had also seen something and needed time to process it. "I wish we'd thought to talk to the other driver," lamented Caroline. But the women were too stunned to think of that. "We were crying and shaking."

Certain that they would not be believed, they agreed to tell no one—not even their husbands. But they couldn't hold it in. "We both told our husbands as soon as we got home," laughed Candy.

They later went back to the scene in the middle of the day. When they found the yard the apparition had strode across, they wondered if he had once lived in the lovely old home. "Then we looked across the street," said Caroline. "There was a funeral home."

Had the ghost originated from *there*? Is it possible that the figure they had seen was a spirit lingering near his body? Was he taking a stroll around the neighborhood as he waited to be buried?

"We researched and found just one man who had died on that day," said Caroline. "But he was in his sixties and the man we'd seen was in his thirties."

This does not discount the possibility that the two are one and the same. Many believe that ghosts can appear as much younger versions of themselves than when they died. The ghost, of course, could have belonged to any number of folks whose bodies were brought to the funeral home in the past.

It is also possible that the ghost belonged to someone who had lived on that street—perhaps someone who was killed while crossing the road.

Though the identity of the spirit is still cloaked in mystery, Caroline and Candy agree that the sighting has had a profound effect on them. "It was a life-altering experience," stressed Caroline, adding that the occurrence inspired her to become more spiritual and get closer to God.

Mirror, Mirror . . .

Marc Moberg, a twenty-one-year-old espresso barista in Puyallup, Washington, told me he has seen a ghost just once in his life. And that one time was enough to make a believer out of him. "It was about seven years ago," he said, describing how he and his mother, Lisa Moberg, had stopped in a flower shop in Buckley, Washington.

Lisa, too, owned a flower shop and was looking for ideas for her business.

The owner of the Buckley store was a friendly woman who greeted them enthusiastically and showed them around. Marc, who was a teenager at the time, perked up when the conversation turned from flowers to something he found far more interesting. *Ghosts!*

"She told us the place had been a funeral home a hundred years before," said Marc, adding that she also shared the fact that ghosts were often seen there. The mystifying sound of organ music sometimes interrupted the silence and unexplained drops of temperature were also experienced. "She took us to the room that used to be the embalming room and the steel table was still there, and there were chains hanging from the ceiling."

Fascinated, Marc began exploring. Near the front of the shop, he peeked into a nook where two mirrors faced each other on opposite walls, giving the effect of a long hallway as they reflected back on each other. "I saw a ghost," he confided. "He looked like he was at the end of a hallway. He wore a black coat and a top hat. He didn't have legs."

Excited, Marc called to his mother, who rushed over to take a look. Lisa Moberg, too, saw the apparition.

The shop owner just smiled. "She wasn't that excited because she'd seen ghosts so many times there," said Marc. In fact, she was so accustomed to the spirits that she didn't bother to cross the room to see the one they had found.

When Marc and Lisa described what they'd seen, she nodded knowingly. "She told us she had seen the same person," said Marc.

The old funeral home is no longer a flower shop, said Marc. Another business now occupies the building and he is planning to stop in someday to see if they, too, have seen the ghosts.

Ghosts on the Road

Phillip Rouss can't help but smile when he remembers how much fun his parents had taking car trips together. "Dad was the regional manager of the United Shoe Machine Company," he said, describing how the senior Phillip's route covered a four-hundred-mile radius near Memphis in the 1960s.

Sadie and Phillip Rouss, Sr., sang along with their Guy Lombardo eight-track tapes and sometimes wrote their own songs to sing in the car as the miles flew by.

They were happy times for Sadie, who, at ninety-two, has spent over a dozen years without her husband. "Dad passed away in 1991," said Phil junior, who is privy to an unusual memory his parents shared. "Dad talked about it till the day he died."

Sadie, too, will never forget the odd encounter on a lovely spring afternoon. She and her husband were driving home from an Atlanta trip and were on Highway 78 about halfway between Holly Springs, Mississippi, and Memphis, Tennessee, when they saw some other travelers who seemed out of place and out of time on the side of the two-lane highway.

"They saw a wagon train," said Phil. They stared at the sight that seemed right out of an old western. An elderly couple sat in the front of the horse-drawn wagon train. The man held the reins, a pipe clenched in his teeth.

"The woman wore a white bonnet," Sadie remembered.

The Rousses were so stunned they traveled two blocks before Phillip senior said, "We have to meet those people!"

Figuring that the unusual travelers must be involved in making a movie, they headed back to the spot where they'd seen them less than two minutes before.

"They were gone," said Sadie, who still shakes her head in awe.

How could the wagon train have vanished so quickly? The couple got out of their car, puzzled. They examined the wet ground, scrutinizing it for the track marks that should surely have been left there but found none.

The Rousses drove around the area, searching for the elusive travelers. They were nowhere to be seen, and there were no nearby roads they could have ducked onto.

"Mom and Dad couldn't wait to get home and tell my sister and me," said Phil.

But when the parents excitedly shared their experience, Phil and his sister mocked them. "Yeah, yeah, yeah," they teased the elder Rousses.

"They got mad at us," Phil said, laughing a little at the memory.

Phil senior and Sadie were shaken by the episode. "I could see the fear in Dad's face," said Phil. They did not know what to make of the odd event. The apparition had been so vivid that they could describe the curl of smoke rising from the old pioneer's pipe, the big black hat on his head, and the rope and the water keg that hung from the side of the wagon.

When they saw their grown kids' reaction to their experience, they extracted a promise from them. "They insisted we never tell anyone about it," said Phil. "They were afraid people would think they were nuts."

Until now, they shared this incredible episode with family only. Sadie is still baffled by the mystery.

Did they see the ghosts of pioneers?

Perhaps.

Or the apparition may have been a place memory, a phenomenon where a dramatic event is inexplicably impressed upon the environment. Like a loop of movie film, it is played back when the conditions are just right.

It is theorized that in such an instance the actual *spirits* of the people seen are not really there—no more than the soul of Clark Gable is present when *Gone with the Wind* is viewed.

If it *was* a ghost encounter, the figures seen could have interacted with witnesses. And if indeed the old pioneers *were* ghosts, they would have been mighty confused by the sight of motor cars whizzing by along with such new-fangled gadgets as eight-track tapes. Time marches on.

Dead Man's Detour

It was a hot summer afternoon in 1995 as twenty-one-year-old Angela Boley headed toward a three o'clock class at the Art Academy of Cincinnati in Ohio. As she drove along Wooster Pike, she noticed something odd. The normally busy road was quiet. In fact, only one other car drove on the road. "It was an ugly tan car from the 1970s," she told me. "It looked like a Buick and it was really loud, like it had a hole in its exhaust. It was covered with big bumper stickers that said things like "Free Ireland."

The car was moving along at about forty miles per hour and she found herself studying the bumper stickers. After a moment she pressed her foot on the gas pedal, moved to the other lane, and left the Buick behind.

She was again alone on the road—until she reached the stoplight. "There was the same ugly car waiting for me at the stoplight! I knew no one had passed me and I had left that car in the dust."

Yet it appeared to be the exact car she had left behind. "All the bumper stickers were the same, it made the same sound, and it had rust in all the same places," she told me.

Angela was baffled. There had been no exits since she passed him— no place for him to have gotten off and sped ahead. How could he have gotten in front of her?

As she pulled up beside him, she glanced through her open window at the teenage driver in the other car. He was a pale skinny boy with short black hair, and he stared straight ahead. The teen was dressed in black, and she noted it was an odd choice for such a warm day. It also struck her that he appeared to be a cautious driver with his hands placed precisely at "eleven o'clock and two o'clock on the steering wheel." He never moved. "He didn't even blink," she remembered.

"A strange feeling came over me," she confided, describing the overwhelming sense of dread. She had the sensation that she should not look at him—that she was seeing something she shouldn't be seeing.

Despite the feeling of foreboding, Angela was not really frightened. She was confused and extremely curious. She kept glancing toward the car as they went through the town of Mariemont, both of them headed toward Columbia Parkway—a stretch of highway notorious for fatal accidents.

"I slowed down as we went through the dangerous 'dead man's curve' on the highway, a near perfect U-shaped bend marked with yellow flashing lights," Angela explained. She watched the other driver and noted, "He didn't even turn the wheel at all as he went through the bend. He was completely immobile! It was like the driver was frozen in time, like a 3-D photograph."

She could not quite wrap her mind around the surreal episode she found herself in. She grasped for logical explanations but there were none. Determined not to lose sight of him, she watched her rearview mirror, but soon he was left behind and she was alone on the road again.

"I thought the car got off at the Red Bank exit, but when I stopped at another stoplight, there was that very same car waiting for me."

It's impossible! she thought. She suddenly found herself thinking of a 1976 hit song by the band Kiss. "It is called 'Detroit Rock City' and it's about a kid killed in a car accident on the way to a concert," she said. Along with the tune, a thought popped into her head. "He's dead. He was killed on this stretch of highway and wants attention. He wants me to follow him."

Prior to this revelation, the word "ghost" had not entered her mind as she tried to sort out the odd occurrence. Now the realization that this was a spirit encounter crystallized.

"I had to turn off to go to Eden Park Drive, but the car continued on Columbia Parkway, and it looked like it was headed straight for downtown Cincinnati," said Angela. "I wanted to follow it to satisfy my curiosity, but I had class."

Nearly nine years have passed since Angela shared the road with the mysterious boy. Today, she still lives in Ohio, and is an artist with a fine arts degree. The surreal journey is etched distinctly in her memory.

Interestingly, it is the stillness of the event that stands out the most. "He was like a statue," she told me, recalling the unblinking apparition with his hands placed so precisely on the steering wheel. The air, too, was eerily still, as if the day were holding its breath.

When Angela expressed regret that she had not followed the freakish car to the end of its journey, I felt an unaccustomed fear. "I'm glad you didn't!" I quickly told her. It occurred to me that if she *had*, she might not be here to tell her story. For it seemed to me that the ghost was not visiting *her* plane, but she was visiting *his*. The fact that all the other traffic vanished from the busy thoroughfare indicated that Angela unknowingly took a paranormal detour.

Probably there were other cars on Wooster Pike and Columbia Parkway on that date and at that time and if we investigated we'd likely find witnesses that would testify that they were traveling there.

Apparently Angela stepped out of our time and space for her meeting with a stuck soul. While most of the ghost encounters I investigate seem to take place when the witnesses have at least one foot planted firmly in this plane, I have interviewed those who seem to completely leave our dimension.

The rules of our plane and our time dissolve in these incidents. While some of the world's greatest minds continue to develop theories on anomalies such as time warps, they have yet to discover definitive answers.

As for the encounter, Angela has her own theory. She believes that the teenage boy was killed on his way to a concert in the 1970s and wants his parents to know that he was not driving recklessly—that the accident was not his fault.

"Maybe if they knew the truth, it would bring them some peace," she said.

Perhaps she is right. Perhaps we will hear from a grieving family who will claim the ghost in the distinctive tan car as their own.

According to Angela, the dangerous curve in the road, long known as "dead man's curve," has been altered so it is not nearly so deadly.

Whenever I think of Angela's inexplicable journey, I get chills. And I wonder if anyone else has taken Columbia Parkway's "dead man's detour."

𝕲𝖍𝖔𝖘𝖙𝖘 𝖎𝖓 𝖙𝖍𝖊 𝕹𝖊𝖜𝖘

OUR HAUNTED HIGHWAYS

Legends of road ghosts can be found in every corner of the planet. Often difficult to validate, these stories are nevertheless told and retold. The following hauntings from the highway have been mentioned in the news:

Going My Way?

FOR THE LAST FOUR DECADES in the Halifax, Nova Scotia, area an eighteen-wheeler truck is said to pick up hitchhikers along Waverly Road. The driver, named Joe, was killed in an accident years ago but that doesn't stop him from giving lifts to unsuspecting riders. Apparently, he tells hitchhikers his full name and they later learn they've taken a spin with a ghost.

(Source: *Halifax Daily News*, April 2002)

Hell Hollow Hello

A DANGEROUS ROAD IN CONNECTICUT is the site of frequent bad accidents and a place where restless spirits roam. The Hell Hollow area of Pachaug State Forest was named for a depression in the woods where two women died. One was a Native American woman who was murdered by British soldiers after they killed her family. Some say her pitiful wailing can still be heard. The other ghost belongs to a suspected witch named Maude, who is restless because her gravestone was stolen.

(Source: New London newspaper *The Day*, September 18, 2003)

Here Comes the Bride

CEDARVALE ROAD IN CEDARVALE, NEW YORK, is legendary as the site of a ghostly bride. An ethereal lady in white appears on the rural road of thirteen curves.

While area skeptics say the ghost story is a hoax, others have stepped forward to describe their encounters—including incidents that go back to the 1950s. Many insist the ghost is that of a bride killed on her wedding night on the twisting road ten miles southwest of Syracuse. When the car missed a curve, it plunged into a creek.

Dolores Collard told a reporter that she had seen the ghost over three decades before while riding in the car with her family. The frightened family thought they were about to hit a pedestrian when they saw the lovely woman in a white gown on the road, but the ghost simply "walked through the car."

Witnesses of more recent sightings say the ghost carries a glowing lantern in her left hand.

(Source: The Associated Press, October 2000)

Ghost Wrecks

FOLKS IN HEREFORDSHIRE, ENGLAND, believe that a victim killed in a car crash is responsible for the unexplained accidents on the A465 near Bromyard. In an eighteen-month period, twenty-six drivers crashed into a fence in the same place. Though the cars often roll in the accidents, no one is injured, which adds to the mystery. Some of the drivers said they had inexplicably lost control of the steering wheel, as if someone were wrestling it away from them. Concerned authorities improved road signs and conducted speed checks but the perplexing crashes continued. The ghost is believed to be that of a woman killed at that spot six decades ago.

(Source: BBC, October 26, 2002)

Vengeance from the Grave

POCAHONTAS PARKWAY in eastern Henrico County, Virginia, is the site of a tollbooth haunted by the ghosts of tribal warriors who are frequently seen, startling drivers into dropping their coins. Both the toll takers and state troopers have become accustomed to reports from motorists who often assume that the torch-carrying warriors are alive. Usually appearing after midnight, the specters ride horses and whoop aggressively.

Some witnesses described the apparitions as fully formed with distinct torsos and fading heads.

A state police spokeswoman who made a late-night visit to the toll plaza was quoted as saying, "Three separate times during our watch, I heard high-pitched howls and screams. Not the kind of screams of a person in trouble, but whooping. There were at least a dozen to fifteen voices. I would say every hair on my body was standing up when we heard those noises."

Before the construction of the parkway, archaeologists sifted through the site and found tribal artifacts that dated back thousands of years.

(Source: *Richmond Times Dispatch*, August 11, 2002)

Author's Note:
This writer's research reveals that the area was once a war zone, with the English and the native Pamunkey tribe fighting for the land. The English set an evil precedent when they kidnapped and murdered native children, a practice that shocked the Pamunkeys. In 1662, Chief Opechancanough orchestrated a massacre on 350 white settlers. Survivors retaliated, killing so many natives and obliterating their tribes that a truce followed and lasted two decades—until an elderly Opechancanough waged war again, killing many before he, too, was murdered.

A Helping Hand

While I have never investigated a case where anyone was physically harmed by a ghost, I've seen instances where spirits have helped people, including the incredible story of the grandfather who reached out from beyond the grave to give a future to new generations. The following story tells of the extraordinary connection between a woman and the grandfather she never knew in life:

It was a hot summer afternoon in Houston, Texas, and five-year-old Dawn sat on her bed, quietly playing with her Barbie dolls. Movement caught her eye and she looked up. There, standing in the hallway, was a man she had never seen before.

"We looked each other up and down," Dawn told me, recalling the distinctive image of the dark-haired man. "He was wearing an undershirt with black pants and shiny black shoes."

She assumed he was simply a visitor but was puzzled when he walked into the bathroom and did not shut the door. "We were taught to *always* shut the door after going into the bathroom," Dawn said.

When the man did not emerge from the bathroom, she grew curious. She investigated but he had vanished. When she reported the visitor to her mother and grandmother, they looked at each other and shook their heads.

It couldn't be!

Dawn had described the grandfather she had never known. "He died before I was born," she explained.

Had she seen his ghost?

When the possibility was raised Dawn's grandmother was adamant. "I don't believe in ghosts," she said flatly.

"But, Googie!" Dawn protested, using her pet name for her grandma. "I *saw* him!"

Today, Dawn Edwards, manager of a video store and mother of an eight-year-old boy, speaks of her grandfather with awe. "He is my guardian angel."

Hubert Clark Scott was a handsome six-foot-tall salesman with a kind heart and a winning sense of humor. After a long battle with cancer, he succumbed months before Dawn was born. Incoherent on his deathbed, he rambled senselessly when Dawn's mother and grandmother visited in the hospital.

"My mother was pregnant with me," explained Dawn. "Everyone was sure I would be a boy because of the way she carried me. They even had a boy's name picked out."

But as Dawn's mother stood by her father's bed, he suddenly spoke in an inexplicable moment of lucidity. He reached out his hand and curled it around her belly. "Take care of my granddaughter," he said. In the next instant he was again confused.

Dawn believes that in that instant she and her grandfather formed a bond that could not be broken. She has sensed him throughout her life.

"He was in World War II," said Dawn. "I wear his dog tags. Whenever I am at a parade, I feel my arm go up to salute the men and women in the service as they walk by. I was never taught to salute. I feel a tingling in my arm as this happens."

It is just one of the dozens of ways that Dawn senses her grandfather beside her. Skeptics might explain these little things away as simply being the product of an overactive imagination. But who can explain what happened to her as she waited in her car at a red light?

"My son and I were both in the car," said Dawn. Suddenly she had the unmistakable sensation of a hand on her chin. "It guided me to look in the rearview mirror."

At the same time, a man's voice shouted, "Look up, damn it!"

Though startled by the disembodied voice, Dawn obeyed and saw a huge dump truck speeding toward them. Quickly she moved the car to the side of the road and an instant later the truck whizzed by. "It would have rear-ended us. At the speed it was going, it could have turned my car into a heap of metal and killed both me and my son."

Dawn says that her experiences with her grandfather's spirit prove to her that there are ghosts among us. "I believe they are good and bad," she said. "I am blessed to have such a loving one. For without him, I would not be here to raise my son and my son might not have lived through the speeding-dump-truck ordeal."

Ghosts in the News

ON FEBRUARY 18, 1999, the *Orlando Sentinel* reported that a ghost saved the life of forty-year-old Maria Tejada in Kissimmee, Florida. Tejada was watching television when she heard her deceased father's voice.

Tejada was quoted as saying, "He told me to get up off the couch. I didn't listen the first two times he said it, but the third time I got up and went over to the loveseat."

It was at that instant that a 1982 Chevy crashed through her front door. The automobile knocked over the couch and demolished an interior wall.

The seventeen-year-old driver and his passenger were en route to school when they took their disastrous detour. The kid claimed his brakes failed but officials found nothing wrong with them. The teen was presented with a ticket for careless driving.

Interestingly, the house had a reputation for being haunted. Neighbors had long gossiped about the slamming doors, strange noises emanating from the attic, and phantom footsteps associated with the home.

Though Tejada insisted it was her father's voice who warned her, she said he was not responsible for the other paranormal activity there. It was, she said, the ghost of a man who had hanged himself in a big oak tree beside the house twenty years before. She and a neighbor had once heard his ghost walking on her roof.

Ghosts in the News

CAN A GHOST ACTUALLY HARM A PERSON? This writer has yet to investigate a case where a person was physically hurt by a ghost. And a United Kingdom insurance company is gambling that it won't happen either.

An April 5, 2002, report by the BBC said that at the request of pub landlord Terry Meggs, the Ultraviolet insurance company wrote a policy to "pay out up to £1m if staff or customers are killed or suffer permanent disability caused by ghosts, poltergeists or other abnormal phenomena on the premises."

According to the news report, the Royal Falcon Hotel in Lowestoff, Suffolk, is next to an old graveyard and Meggs grew concerned when "he saw the ghost shoot glasses along the bar one night."

Meggs pays a premium of five hundred pounds for the peace of mind of knowing he will be covered if a patron is harmed by a spirit.

Housed in a five-hundred-year-old building, the Royal Falcon Hotel was once the Eastholme Girls School. It is purported to be haunted "by a monk who hanged himself after being caught having an affair with one of the pupils or teachers."

The BBC said the Ultraviolet insurance company covers "a range of paranormal activity."

The report concluded by saying that several years ago Ultraviolet paid out 100,000 pounds on its "Spooksafe policy." The insurance company claimed that an American woman died after being thrown over the banister of her home. The BBC said it was "concluded that a ghost was responsible for the crime."

This writer remains skeptical.

The Joke Is on You

Though I haven't researched a case where a ghost did bodily harm to a person, I've interviewed people who have shared their homes with menacing presences. Though the threat of harm is there, no one has actually been hurt. The following story tells of a spooky encounter one family had with an unseen entity:

Elizabeth Wilson was sixteen in 1972 when her mother moved her and her four siblings into a rental house in Skykomish, Washington. "It was a shabby brown two-story house," Elizabeth remembered with a shudder. "It was haunted. You can ask my brothers and sister and they'll tell you the same thing! I get goose bumps just talking about it."

The house was about a century old. "It had once been the head-quarters for the Apex gold mine," she explained.

The historic town in northwestern Washington is known both for the railroads that ran through it and for the gold mine once harvested there.

While the sisters each had their own room downstairs, the three boys shared the huge open space of the second floor. While some girls might think it is a luxury to have their own rooms, Elizabeth and her eleven-year-old sister, Alyce, were not thrilled with the arrangement.

Each night as Elizabeth turned off her light, she snuggled under the covers only to be disturbed by a cold whoosh of wind. "It rushed right over me, lifting my hair," she remembered. "It was the most eerie feeling!"

"I began to sleep with the light on," she said, explaining that the mysterious gust blew past her only in the dark.

Little Alyce was not faring too well in her room either. A presence also visited her in the night. "She said a little girl came and talked to her," said Elizabeth.

Elizabeth soon learned from neighbors that they were not the only tenants to be frightened by the house. "The family who lived there before us had a little boy who would not allow anyone to shut the door to his room when he was in there," said Elizabeth. "He would cry and tell his parents that there was someone in the room with him."

While Elizabeth and her siblings did not like to be scared, they enjoyed scaring others. In fact, they loved to play practical jokes. "We bought a mannequin head at a thrift shop," she remembered. "It looked real." It was a woman's head with rooted blonde hair and "wicked staring eyes."

The pranksters stuck the head on the antenna of the car and drove around town. "We almost caused a few accidents," Elizabeth sheepishly admitted.

The kids may have thought they were pretty clever, but the joke was on *them*. For one evening all of the kids were downstairs when they heard a hollow thud. Thud. Thud. Thud.

The kids looked at each other, baffled by the noise. "It sounded like something was rolling down the stairs. And then it rolled back *up*!"

When the noise stopped, they went to investigate. "We found the mannequin head had been moved. And it was not the last time it happened," remembered Elizabeth. Several more times, the head was heard bouncing around upstairs. "We finally got rid of it."

Alyce, who was small for an eleven-year-old, had a favorite prank she liked to play on her older sister's unsuspecting friends. An old player piano with its insides missing occupied one wall of Elizabeth's room. Alyce was petite enough to climb inside and would often do so when no one was looking. As soon as the older girls were engrossed in conversation, the mischievous little girl would pluck the piano keys.

"It made a 'dink, dink, dink,' sound," said Elizabeth. "She always made the exact same sound." Elizabeth, of course, would just laugh when she heard the familiar pattern but the sudden playing of the piano startled her friends.

Then one evening as the family was eating at the dinner table, they heard it. "Dink, dink, dink."

Alyce up to her old tricks?

Not exactly.

All eyes went to Alyce, who sat with them at the table. Realization sunk in. "We were all there," Elizabeth remembered. "And we were stunned when we saw she was there too!"

Who had hit the distinctive pattern of notes?

"We got up to investigate," said Elizabeth. They peered inside the piano. No one was inside.

Once again, the joke was on them!

"Alyce never played that trick again," said Elizabeth with a laugh.

Who was the mysterious prankster who seemed to join in on the kids' jokes?

Perhaps the culprit was nothing more than a kid herself. For the presence who visited Alyce's room often cried like a little girl. Alyce heard her many times.

"Mommy! Mommy!" The cries were stained with tears.

Who was the ghost?

The puzzle was solved when Elizabeth chatted with neighbors—old-timers who had lived in the area a long time. "They told me that a little girl had died of pneumonia in the house," she said, explaining the death occurred somewhere around the early 1900s.

Was the troubled little spirit the only ghost haunting the home? Or did other ghosts reside there too? No one, of course, can say for sure. But some of the paranormal occurrences chilled the children to the marrow. Elizabeth shivered as she recalled an incident in the kitchen. "We had one of those old wringer washing machines," she said. "One day my sister was standing in the kitchen when the washing machine lifted five inches off the floor."

Several family members watched in horror as the machine levitated, then tilted toward the little girl as if it were going to dump water on her.

Was it just another prank by a troubled little ghost? Or was there something more sinister at the home?

The answers are ashes in the wind.

A few years after the family moved out, the house was burned down as a practice exercise for local firefighters.

Time Is on My Side
(BUT WHAT ABOUT "THE *OTHER* SIDE"?)

Tick tock. Tick tock.

Time.

We know it as a measurable, linear thing. Night follows day. July follows June. Noon never comes before 11 A.M.

This is how things are in our world. But on "the *other* side" things may be different. Imagine if time were out of sequence. What if a century felt like a second and yesterday happened after tomorrow?

A ghost possibly has one foot in a place where the rules of *our* reality disintegrate. He straddles two dimensions—our rigid world of precise measurements and a realm where walls *and time* do not exist.

This theory explains why a ghost might haunt a tiny, smelly shack for ninety years.

People shake their heads and ask, "Why in the world would he stick around for so long when there is a whole wonderful universe to explore?"

This author answers, "Because to the ghost it may not be long at all! A century could be just a blink of an eye."

B&B&G

(Bed-and-Breakfast and *Ghost!*)

The Lemp Mansion and the Legend of the Monkey Boy

The day before I left for St. Louis, Missouri, I had learned just three things about the city's famous Lemp Mansion. It had originally belonged to a family who made their fortune in the lager beer business. *Life* magazine had once featured it as one of the ten most haunted places in the United States.

And it was haunted by the ghost of the Monkey Boy!

The Monkey Boy was believed to be the spirit of a deformed child, trapped indefinitely in the attic of what is now a restaurant and bed-and-breakfast.

Though I pride myself on never being frightened of ghosts, I must admit that my enthusiasm was somewhat dampened when I called to make reservations and owner Patty Pointer told me that I would be the only person staying there. "The staff goes home at three P.M. on Wednesdays," she explained, and cheerfully added, "And you'll be our only guest here that night. You'll have the mansion all to yourself to explore."

"All alone?"

All alone with the Monkey Boy!

"Yes, but there is one problem," Patty said. "You'll need to get the key before we leave."

My plane would not be arriving until after six, so I contacted fellow ghost author Troy Taylor for help. It was his invitation that lured me to the area, as I would be speaking in his Alton, Illinois, bookstore the following Saturday.

"You must know a reliable woman or two who would like to have a haunted slumber party," I suggested.

Violent death within the Lemp Mansion is believed to be responsible for making this B&B the most haunted spot in St. Louis. (Leslie Rule)

He certainly did and soon the arrangements were made.

Anita Dytuco and her daughter, twenty-two-year-old Amy, picked me up at the airport. We went out for dinner and they told me they had picked up the key and later dropped their overnight bags off at the Lemp Mansion. "I turned on all the lights downstairs as a test," said Amy, explaining that many have reported that lights at the mansion turn off and on by themselves.

Sure enough, when we arrived at the big house we found that the lights had been turned off in two rooms. "Someone could be playing a trick on us," I said as I flipped the switches back on.

But Amy was scared. She followed tentatively as we explored. The thirty-three-room mansion boasts high ceilings, impossibly tall door-ways, ornate antique fixtures, and vintage decor. The street level and the basement serve as the restaurant, while the third floor and part of the attic house overnight guests.

(Left to right) Amy Dytuco, Anita Dytuco, and Bonnie Kleiss pause on the stairway at the Lemp Mansion. Before their visit was over, two of these women would encounter ghosts. (Leslie Rule)

It took some urging for us to convince Amy to explore the attic. Armed with flashlights, we crept up the narrow back staircase, once used by servants, past the attic's renovated area, down a long hallway, and into a dark cramped space. It was in this hot, stuffy place that the help had lived. While the Lemp family occupied the opulent, spacious rooms below, the servants' quarters were divided into closet-sized spaces with tiny floor-level windows.

The legend of the Monkey Boy began decades earlier when neighbors whispered that they had seen an ape-like child peering at them from the small attic windows. A rumor spread that Billy Lemp, a married grandson of founder Adam Lemp, had romanced a maid and that the unfortunate child was a result of the forbidden union. The boy was exiled forever to the attic.

It really wasn't a very scary idea. It was sad.

Our attic expedition yielded nothing exciting. The batteries in our flashlights went prematurely dead as we were exploring—a common phenomenon in haunted sites—and we fumbled our way out. Only one of our trio was to have a paranormal experience before the adventure was over, but it would not be until dawn's soft light embraced the mansion.

As for the Monkey Boy, he did not appear. Was there such a child? Many have searched for documentation of his existence but proof has yet to be found. The reputedly most haunted mansion in St. Louis, however, has no shortage of tragic stories to feed its ghost legend.

The story begins in the mid–nineteenth century when the city's natural underground caverns enticed German brewers who found them perfect for refrigeration. Adam Lemp built his empire above a long, rambling cave, which eventually connected the lager beer brewery to the family home.

The beer business boomed and the Lemps' fortune was made.

In 1876, Adam's son, William J. Lemp, moved his wife, Julia, and six children into the big Italianate structure. The kids were all under the age of ten and the huge home's halls must have rung with laughter as Anna, William junior, Louis, Charles, Frederick, and Hilda frolicked and played. When Edwin was born in 1880 and then Elsa in 1883, the family was complete.

During that year wealthy children played with Steiff teddy bears,

This old postcard depicts the impressive Lemp Brewery when business was booming. Underground tunnels connect it to the Lemp Mansion. (Courtesy of the Ronald Snowden Collection)

exquisite-faced porcelain dolls, wooden blocks, and marbles and rode straw-stuffed horses on wheels. The Lemp children's nursery, believed to have been located in the third-floor tower room at the top of the main staircase, was certainly filled with the finest toys. I hope these were happy times for the children, for their lives were later marred by tragedy.

Their father set a dark precedent when he took his own life in 1904. He shot himself in the mansion. His son, William J., Jr., followed suit, killing himself in the same room eighteen years later, in 1922. His brother, Charles Lemp, committed suicide in a basement room in 1949.

Though there are four deaths in the Lemp family documented as suicide, one is particularly suspicious. Elsa, the littlest Lemp, born and raised in the Lemp Mansion, died from a "self-inflicted" gunshot wound in 1920.

When she married Thomas Wright, she was the wealthiest single woman in St. Louis. On the tragic day, she was thirty-six years old and lived with him in a grand home on Hortense Place. She had been suffering one of her mysterious bouts of stomach problems the March morning she died.

"She said she was feeling better," said Thomas Wright.

Was she simply depressed over her illness, as her husband had insisted?

Or was the loss of her only child too much to bear? Baby Patricia had died six years earlier on the day she was born.

Or did someone else have a hand in Elsa's death?

Thomas had remarried the heiress to the Lemp fortune just eleven days before, after an earlier divorce that kept them separated for about a year.

The *St. Louis Dispatch* reported that on the morning of March 20, Elsa was in bed when Thomas headed for the shower. When he heard the gunshot he went back to the bedroom and found Elsa wounded. He shouted for help and the maid came running. Elsa died shortly after.

An inquest concluded the death was a suicide. Yet the recent remarriage raised questions. Was the couple happy together? Why would Elsa kill herself when she was feeling better? And what was the cause of her stomach ailment?

If this tragedy unfolded today, the coroner would certainly have looked for poison.

Murder or suicide, it was indeed a troubling death—the kind of death that often results in earthbound spirits. If anyone had an attachment to the Lemp Mansion, it would be Elsa, who was born and raised there.

Neighbors said the Monkey Boy peered out of the small attic windows where he was confined. Does his ghost still reside in the attic of the Lemp Mansion? (Leslie Rule)

Both male and female ghosts have been seen at the Lemp Mansion.

A waitress was setting up one morning when she spotted an early customer sitting at one of the tables. "Would you like some coffee?" she asked as she approached him. The man stared into space, ignoring her. A moment later, he vanished.

Was it one of the Williamses, Charles, or Frederick, the favorite son who worked so hard on the family business he dropped dead of heart failure in his late twenties? His heiress, daughter Marion, was later denied a fair share of the Lemp fortune despite the fact Frederick had done more for the business than his siblings. A lawsuit was filed on twelve-year-old Marion's behalf, but most of her aunts and uncles fought her and won. As a result, Frederick would certainly have reason to be a disgruntled spirit.

As for the female presence, visitors to the Lemp Mansion like to think she is Lillian Handlan, ex-wife of William junior and affectionately known as "The Lavender Lady." The vivacious socialite was so adored by city folk that crowds met her train whenever she returned from a trip. Dubbed "The Lavender Lady" during the highly publicized divorce trial from Billy Lemp, who cited his wife's love for the color as one of the reasons for the divorce, Lillian staunchly protested the accusation. The newspaper quoted her as saying in court, "I've never worn lavender in my life."

While fans of the Lemp Mansion count "The Lavender Lady" among the ghosts there, this writer is skeptical. She was not fond of the home, and though she hosted parties there she never actually resided at the mansion and died elsewhere at age seventy-three.

I believe it is *Elsa* who looks after the Lemp Mansion. The youngest of the Lemp children, she spent her entire childhood there. More than anyone, she would certainly have an attachment to the place.

Another clue strengthens the possibility.

Today the Lemp Mansion is famous for its "Murder Mystery Dinners" where actors add drama to mealtime with first-rate performances of fascinating characters involved in a crime. These actors use the Lemp nursery for their costume room and many report odd occurrences. One actress told me of a sighting that brings poor Elsa to mind. An old-fashioned baby buggy, apparently stored in the nursery, suddenly bolted

Nooks and crannies and secret tunnels are filled with ghosts at the spooky Lemp Mansion. (Leslie Rule)

out of the empty room and shot into the hallway as if invisible hands had pushed it.

Did those ethereal hands belong to Elsa? And did the buggy hold the ghost of her infant daughter Patricia?

It is an interesting question to ponder.

The Pointer family has owned the Lemp Mansion since 1975 and most have experienced odd activity since.

Bonnie Kleiss, Patty Pointer's college-age niece, will never forget the chill she felt many years ago. "I was about six and my grandma asked me to go upstairs and get some keys for her," she told me. "Right as I got to the top of the grand staircase, I heard a man's voice."

He spoke just one word. "Bonnie."

"I ran as fast as I could back downstairs and never gave an explanation as to why I didn't get the keys. I never told anyone in my family about what I had heard."

Bonnie showed up to stay at the Lemp Mansion on my second day there, and it was then that she confided in me about her experience with the disembodied voice. Later, when I was back home, I received an e-mail from her. It had happened *again*!

This time she was in bed in the Charles Lemp Suite. As she was drifting off to sleep, a young man's voice intruded on her slumber. "The difference between this one and the one I heard years ago was that this time it was more playful, 'Bohh-nniee,' like it was calling out to me. When I first heard this, it was stated more matter-of-factly."

It was almost as if the ghost had *heard* Bonnie tell me the story and was teasing her.

Though the ghosts of the Lemp Mansion didn't speak to *me*, they were in a talkative mode during my stay, for Bonnie wasn't the only one who heard them.

Sweet Amy Dytuco, the terrified member of our little slumber party, also heard from a Lemp ghost! She was so scared that she slept cuddled up to her mother in the big bed in the lovely Lavender Suite. "I couldn't sleep all night," she confessed. And then, just as the night was dissolving, a kind female voice whispered, "It's going to be all right." The words were gentle and loving and so soothing that Amy was swept into a peaceful sleep.

The Lemp Mansion in St. Louis, Missouri, has converted many ghost skeptics to believers. (Leslie Rule)

Who spoke to Amy? It wasn't Anita. She was fast asleep.

As I pored over the guest books signed by past Lemp guests, I noted a recurrent theme. Guests had recorded many of their paranormal experiences. Furniture was inexplicably moved. "A toilet screamed." (Perhaps that one wasn't paranormal but a plumbing problem!) Lights were turned off and on. Apparitions were seen.

And there, recorded in ballpoint pen, was an experience so similar to Amy's that I caught my breath. A man wrote that he had spent a night in the Lavender Suite and because of emotional turmoil could not sleep. Late into the night, a kind spirit spoke to him. "It's going to be okay."

And just as Amy had, the troubled man felt an instant peace and finally fell asleep.

Elsa.

Who else could it be? No one, of course, knows for sure, but Elsa Lemp Wright has my vote. If you visit the Lemp Mansion, say hello to her for me!

THE LEMP MANSION
3322 DEMENIL PLACE
ST. LOUIS, MO 63118
(314) 644-8024
WWW.LEMPMANSION.COM

More B&B&Gs

Ivy House Inn

A city called Casper is sure to have its share of ghosts! The Ivy House Inn is a favorite haunt for visitors to the area. When Tom and Kathy Johnson bought the 1916 Cape Cod house and proceeded to turn it into a bed-and-breakfast, they soon realized previous tenants had not left! During renovation, boards flew across the room, objects inexplicably vanished, and the cord to a drill unplugged and floated in the air.

Guests and family members alike have seen the ghost of Mrs. White, the previous owner, who died at ninety-three. She has been spotted walking in the hallway, and once Eric, the couple's teenage son, saw her in his room. Mrs. White materialized, appearing as vivid and as solid as a live human being. He watched, startled, as the old woman powdered her face before vanishing.

Other sightings include Mrs. White's Siamese cat, and a man in a flannel shirt who carries a board.

The Johnsons host an annual Haunted Slumber Party and report that during the event "presences have always made themselves known."

IVY HOUSE INN
815 SOUTH ASH STREET
CASPER, WY 82601
(307) 265-0974
WWW.IVYHOUSEINN.COM

Hickory Grove Inn

The Greek Revival–styled farmhouse overlooking Ostego Lake was purchased by the Curpier family as an abandoned property in 1999. Abandoned?

Not exactly!

"We think there are many ghosts here," admitted owner Marie Curpier, who suspected the Cooperstown, New York, property was haunted from the first moment she saw it. "I knew instantly something was there."

"We don't know exactly when the house was built," explained Marie. "The earliest date we have of its existence is 1830, though it is possible it is over two hundred years old."

The charming house with the wood-beamed ceilings, fieldstone fireplace, and huge inviting front porch was long known as Hickory Grove Inn, a favorite lakeside inn and restaurant, before Matthew and Marie Curpier turned it into a B&B. It is the restaurant spirits that first made their presence known late one freezing January night when Marie and Matthew were sleeping. "I heard a man yawning," said Marie. "It was so loud, it woke me up." The sound emanated from the living room below, which had at one time housed the eatery. "There is no insulation between the floors. You could hear a pin drop."

"At first we thought someone had broken in," explained Marie. The noise escalated and the couple huddled together, listening to the clatter of silverware. "It was as if a busboy was shaking a big cup of silverware," said Marie, who was baffled by the noise. "There was no silverware in that room!"

The clamor included the clanking of dishes, stomping, and drawers banging. "It continued for forty-five minutes and we finally decided to leave."

The Curpiers bundled up and hurried to their car. A soft frosting of snow coated the ground and as they sat shivering in the driveway, Matthew decided to check around the house. He circled the house and found no footsteps in the snow.

Their intruders were not human—at least not *living* humans.

The Curpiers are no longer afraid. "I put my foot down and told the ghosts that they must respect our family," Marie told me, insisting that the spirits are amicable.

Their pranks are harmless. The washer and dryer sometimes turn themselves off and on all night. A shower once turned itself off repeatedly while a guest was using it. Doors slam by themselves and lights go on and off on their own.

Who are the ghosts that haunt the Hickory Grove Inn?

A two-century-old house has plenty of time to gather ghostly inhabitants. Marie wonders if the naughty spirits might belong to the very first family to reside there. "There's a graveyard on the hill behind the house," she said. "The family had thirteen children and some of them died young."

HICKORY GROVE INN BED AND BREAKFAST
6855 STATE HIGHWAY 80
COOPERSTOWN, NY 13326
(607) 547-1313
WWW.HICKORYGROVEINN.COM

Thornewood Castle

An imposing mansion turned bed-and-breakfast in Lakewood, Washington, counts three resident ghosts—including that of a small child who is seen standing beside the nearly lake. When guests spot the little one as they look out their windows, they run to report their concern for the child. The owners smile sadly and shake their heads. The child drowned decades ago.

Many people have prayed for the tiny spirit and believe that the child "went to heaven" and it is simply a place memory left behind.

Castle owners Wayne and Deanna Robinson point to another place memory frequently experienced there.

The haunted Thornewood Castle so impressed horror writer Stephen King that he used it for the movie set for his miniseries Rose Red. *(Leslie Rule)*

Who knows who lurks in the shadows of the Thornewood Castle? This Lakewood, Washington, bed-and-breakfast is famous as a haunted hot spot. (Leslie Rule)

The ghost of a little girl is sometimes seen wandering by the water near the Thornewood Castle. Those in the know say that the child drowned decades ago. (Leslie Rule)

The Thornewood Castle is named for Chester Thorne, who designed his fifty-four-room dream home in the early 1900s to resemble an old English estate. One of the ghosts seen there is thought to be Chester's wife, Anna Hoxie Thorne, who died on January 28, 1954, at the age of eighty-seven.

"In Anna's suite, three different brides have seen the spirit of an elderly woman," said Deanna. "Each time the ghost was seen, the brides were standing before the mirror, looking at themselves in their wedding gowns." The ghost sat on the window seat, watching them.

Other paranormal activity includes glass inexplicably shattering and the recorded voice of a little girl singing caught on tape.

Reservations are required to visit the Thornewood Castle.

THORNEWOOD CASTLE INN AND GARDENS
8601 NORTH THORNE LANE S.W.
LAKEWOOD, WA 98498
(253) 584-4393
WWW.THORNEWOODCASTLE.COM

Oak Alley Plantation

Oak Alley Plantation is a majestic historic estate named for its enormous oaks, which flank the path leading to the antebellum mansion. Planted in the early 1700s, the native trees thrived, creating an "alley" of oaks so visually appealing they've attracted filmmakers for decades. Parts of Bette Davis's 1964 classic thriller *Hush . . . Hush, Sweet Charlotte* were filmed outside the grand mansion.

Visitors can take a tour of the mansion, dine in the estate's restaurant, or—if they are brave enough—stay in one of the cottages on the grounds in a B&B package.

Some say they've seen "the lady in black." Legend has it that she is the ghost of a lady who had an unfortunate accident on the plantation. Trying to thwart the unwanted advances of an inebriated Romeo, the frightened girl ran from him. She tumbled down the stairs and cut her leg so badly that it was amputated and buried on the grounds.

The ghost of a restless young girl is said to search the grounds of the Oak Alley Plantation for something she wants back. (Leslie Rule)

When her lonely form is seen roaming the estate, some surmise that she is looking for her missing leg.

Paranormal activity is frequently reported there—such as the time that thirty-five tourists witnessed a candlestick fly across a room during a tour.

OAK VALLEY PLANTATION, RESTAURANT & INN

3645 HIGHWAY 18 (GREAT RIVER ROAD)

VACHERIE, LA 70090

(225) 265-2151

(800) 44ALLEY

WWW.OAKALLEYPLANTATION.COM

The Victorian Rose

The Victorian Rose. What a perfectly lovely name for a bed–and–breakfast!

The name is *so* perfect that at least a dozen other proprietors across America have chosen it for *their* B&Bs. These other establishments might be wonderful in their own ways, but the Victorian Rose in Ventura, California, is extraordinary. It is housed in a beautiful 1880s church with a classic bell tower and a ninety-six-foot-tall steeple.

The ceilings soar and the stained-glass windows throw a palette of richly colored light on the sweet-faced cherubs and angels that adorn the interior.

Owners Richard and Nona Bogatch devoted two years to restoring the church to a welcoming place that would leave their guests awestruck. While their guests are indeed amazed, it is not just the beauty of the place that astonishes them. Sometimes it is the *ghosts*.

Richard has had countless reports from guests who have seen the spirits who share his home. "We never ask guests if they've seen a ghost," he told me, explaining that they wait until the guests come down for breakfast and bring it up themselves. "If they've seen something, they'll let us know."

Often stunned visitors sip their morning coffee, eyes wide, as they describe their encounters with "a man of the cloth."

The ghostly minister seems to look after the guests. "He tucks them in and strokes their hair," Richard confided, and explained that visitors regard them more as guardian angels than ghosts.

Actually, there may be *two* minister spirits, as the clergy ghosts have been given two different descriptions. One rarely seen ghost is bald, while the other has hair. Both wear the traditional collar. It could, of course, be one spirit appearing at times as he looked when young and other times as he was when he'd aged.

"This was originally a Methodist church," said Richard. Later it was a Baptist church before a religious sect occupied the building.

Sometimes a minister's apparition materializes in the mirror; other times he is seen standing over a bed, smiling benignly at a startled guest.

While Richard has never actually seen a ghost, he has had some odd experiences, including the time he was making a bed. A pillow flew out of the armoire and sailed past him across the room. Was it a member of the clergy who instigated the pillow fight, or perhaps someone else trying to catch his attention?

While the ministers' ghosts are fascinating subjects, there is another soul there that the living still mourn for. She, too, is a sweet spirit but likely is restless. Her life was taken from her long before she was ready.

She has been patient for over two decades, waiting for justice. If you too, dear reader, will also be patient, her shocking story will unfold in the next chapter.

THE VICTORIAN ROSE
896 EAST MAIN STREET
VENTURA, CA 93001
(805) 641-1888
WWW.VICTORIAN-ROSE.COM

When Justice Is Done

We see countless cases of haunted sites where murders have occurred. Murder seems to be the ultimate ghost maker. Nearly as mysterious as the spirits who remain earthbound as a result of this most unjust of deaths, killers are enigmas no one yet completely understands.

There are, of course, people who kill out of self-defense or to protect loved ones. And there are those who simply lose control—are truly insane because of a malfunctioning brain.

Then there are the killers who have no heart. They are so intent on their selfish needs or desires that they can snuff out another human and feel no more guilt than if they swatted a fly. These are the ones who baffle the rest of us.

As mentioned earlier, my mother is true-crime author Ann Rule. She has documented over 1,400 murder cases, has lectured to the FBI, and is considered one of the world's top experts on serial killers. She can think like a police officer. Indeed, she was one for a short while when she was very young but was drummed off the force because of her poor vision. It may surprise some to know that she believes in ghosts. In fact, she has frequently become aware of paranormal occurrences surrounding the cases she covers.

Murder and ghosts go hand in hand. If a killer thinks it is the end when he or she slays another person, they may be in for a rude surprise.

Killers don't deserve the ink it takes to cover these pages, but they are an integral part of some of the following stories, so they must be mentioned here. And *maybe*, just *maybe*, a potential murderer may read these words and decide that taking another's life will not be worth it. Perhaps killers will understand that they don't have any power in the end—that their victims aren't really gone and they will one day have to face them, perhaps in this lifetime.

As Ann's daughter, I've been exposed to killers. And as her photographer since the age of seventeen, I've accompanied her to many trials and sometimes felt those killers' rage as I pointed my camera at them.

I was just a teenager when I took a photo of a beautiful murderess during a courtroom break. She did not look like the paid "hit man" she was. She was petite with thick dark hair that cascaded down her back. I snapped a picture as she puffed on her cigarette, and her eyes turned to granite as she hissed, "I told you not to take a picture of me while I was smoking."

Yes, she had told me that, but I was nervous and forgot. I will always remember that instant when she fixed her venomous eyes upon me. Her stare was the same as the one I received from Randy Roth (a man convicted of killing his third wife and suspected of pushing his second wife off a cliff, both for the insurance money) when I photographed him in the corridor outside the courtroom.

When a killer looks at you like that, it feels as if they have touched your heart with an icy finger. The resulting shiver travels all the way to your toes.

While some murderers have fixed their dark eyes upon me angrily as I snap their photos, others have primped and posed for me.

When killer David Brown saw me with my camera in the Orange County, California, courtroom, he turned away for just a second and pulled out a comb. After neatening his greasy black hair, he turned back and struck a pose as naturally as if he were a celebrity. Far from being an attractive movie star, the stubby man with the pockmarked face was finally on trial for murder. Five years earlier, he had manipulated his fourteen-year-old daughter, Cinnamon, into killing his wife—her twenty-three-year-old stepmother.

The victim, Linda Brown, was a lovely, kind woman and a first-time new mother. Her infant daughter was in the next room and Linda snoozed peacefully as Cinnamon Brown shot her on the night of March 19, 1985.

David Brown had lied to his daughter and told her that Linda was plotting to kill *him*. He convinced her that she had to kill her stepmother or that *he* would die. The fourteen-year-old girl was terrified and did as her father instructed.

In reality, David Brown was having an affair with his wife's seventeen-year-old sister, Patti, and had also involved her in the murder plot. He had taken out a large insurance policy on Linda's life. His plan worked for a while. Cinnamon was imprisoned for the murder. David and Patti and Linda's baby daughter went back to the murder house on Ocean Breeze Drive to wait for the insurance settlement.

Yet things were not quite as they expected. Linda was still there.

The couple could not bring themselves to sleep in the bed where Linda had been murdered. They dragged a mattress out into the recreation room and slept there, where Linda's photograph still smiled down from the mantel.

They could not, however, sleep peacefully. They could hear Linda crying.

They were so tormented by the weeping of the woman they had killed that they could not stay in the house and soon moved out.

When I am not available, my mom often takes her own photographs for her books. When she photographed the murder house on Ocean Breeze Drive, she didn't notice anything unusual—until she got the photo developed.

She slipped it out of the envelope and gasped. There, framed in the front window, was the shape of a woman with long blonde hair.

Linda?

The new residents were Asian with black hair. None of them resembled the young woman who was killed there. It was not one of them standing at the window. "The figure appeared to be between the Venetian blinds and the window," said Ann. "There's no way a human could fit there. She studied the photograph, wondering if it were possible that she had photographed Linda's ghost. Or did she simply capture an odd reflection in the window?

"I went back at the same time of day and tried to duplicate the photo, but I couldn't," Ann said. "I think it is Linda's ghost."

We can't say for certain if the photo shows Linda's ghost. But the phantom weeping heard by David and Patti indicates that her spirit was earthbound for at least a little while. I picture the spirit of the distraught young mother searching for the infant daughter she adored.

That baby girl is grown now.

Justice was served to David Brown. When Cinnamon finally revealed the truth, he was arrested and convicted of murder. He will serve life in prison.

Let's hope Linda is free.

The Last Laugh

When Anne Marie Fahey vanished from Wilmington, Delaware, in 1996, she left scores of grieving friends and a devastated family. The girl with the wonderfully loud carefree laugh was much loved.

At thirty, she should have had many years of happiness ahead, but these were viciously stolen from her by the man she had once loved. Thomas Capano, a well-known attorney from a wealthy Wilmington family, refused to give Anne Marie her freedom. Rather than let her go, he shot her and, with the help of his brother, "buried" her at sea in a cooler.

The killer must have been smug, thinking he had gotten away with taking her vibrant life. But against all odds, a key piece of evidence literally surfaced and put him on death row.

Seventy-five miles out in the Atlantic Ocean, in an area called Shark Alley, Tom Capano dumped the cooler with the lifeless body inside. He thought that both Anne Marie and the cooler-turned-coffin were gone forever.

When investigators learned of the existence of the missing cooler, they knew they needed it to convict Tom Capano. But the odds of it being located were akin to finding a lost grain of sand in the Mohave Desert.

The laws of nature dictate that the cooler should have been carried on currents that traveled far, far away and forever lost in a vast ocean. Though Anne Marie's body was no longer inside, the cooler inexplicably drifted to within a few hundred feet of the Delaware shore, where a fisherman rescued it. When he saw the pink-tinged water inside, he figured the blood was from fish. He happened to have an exact top that matched that style cooler. When he saw the bullet hole in the cooler, he plugged it with resin. Months later, a friend told him he had heard on the news that investigators were searching for an identical cooler. The fisherman notified the police and the cooler was used to convict Thomas Capano.

It was against all odds that that cooler should end up in the hands of law enforcement. It was against the laws of the currents that it should end up bobbing in the waves so close to the shore, where Anne Marie had once wiggled her toes in the sand.

Anne Marie Fahey had a kind heart and a wonderful laugh. Did she have a hand in catching her killer from "the other side"? (From her "missing" poster)

How in the world did that happen?

Ann Rule, who chronicled Anne Marie Fahey's story, said, "I believe that Anne Marie's hand had a part in that."

It warms the heart to think that the girl with the wonderful laugh may have had the last laugh after all.

What makes an innocent little child grow up to be a killer? And what makes another child grow up to be a best-selling true-crime author?

It is that *first* question that results in the answer to the second. At least in my mother's case. Her voyage into the curious depths of the killer mind is prompted by her need to learn what makes a killer. She wants to know *why.*

As my mom and I were recently e-mailing each other about killers and ghosts and our destiny in writing about them, I wrote to her, "You are so tightly woven into this thread. It is almost as if the hand of God plucked you up and put you there, twisting your fate so tightly into this that you could not untangle yourself, even if you wanted to."

Many of you who read this book already know the story of my mother and her friendship with one of the most infamous serial killers our nation has seen. You may not, however, have pondered the possibility that Ted Bundy left dozens of ghosts in the wake of his rage. No one knows exactly how many he killed. Some of his victims have yet to be found. I suspect their restless spirits wander near their gravesites.

This story began for me when I was four years old, in 1962. In one of those moments that crystallizes and settles permanently in the memory, my mother's friend Madge Olson,* from her childbirth education group, pulled into our driveway and rolled down her window to share some shocking news.

Her twelve-year-old daughter, Sue,* had been cut thirteen times. I listened, confused. I knew Sue, though it was her younger siblings I played with when we visited their home.

"Thirteen times! Oh my God!" my mother gasped.

At four, I pictured Sue being cut on a tuna fish can and I remember thinking that she must have been awfully careless to cut herself thirteen times.

But Sue had not cut *herself.* Someone else had cut her. I was stunned when the situation was explained to me.

Sue and her little brother, Jimmy,* had been picking berries when a mailman attacked the twelve-year-old and stabbed her. Selflessly she had screamed to her three-year-old brother, "*Run,* Jimmy! Run home!"

The boy obeyed and a family friend spotted him on the side of the road and gave him a ride. Jimmy was silent the entire way but the instant he walked into his house, he announced, "Sue is dead."

Sue wasn't dead. She miraculously survived the attack and it was soon learned that the deranged letter carrier, afraid he would hurt someone, had tried to seek help for his urges. But there had been nowhere to turn.

The Olson family spearheaded the founding of the Seattle Crisis Clinic. They visualized a place with a hotline where troubled people

---

* Whenever an asterisk appears, names have been changed to protect privacy.

could call twenty-four hours a day. They hoped that a kind voice answering the phone could help someone like the disturbed mailman and avert another tragedy as well as assist those contemplating suicide.

The Seattle Crisis Clinic became a reality in 1971. Ironically, they hired serial killer Ted Bundy to answer the phone. I can't help but wonder if he ever got a call from someone who could not control his violent urges. And if so, what advice did Ted give?

The Crisis Clinic administrators are not at fault for hiring Ted. He was a charismatic young law student who had worked as an aide for Washington state governor Dan Evans.

They had no inkling of the monster inside.

By the strangest of coincidences, Ted was teamed up with my mom, who volunteered her time two nights a week. Her only sibling had committed suicide, and still haunted by the fact that she was not able to save him, she decided to try to help others. She was a busy divorced mother of four, who wrote two to three true-crime articles for detective magazines each week, but felt this was something she *had* to do.

She raved about Ted, the twenty-four-year-old young man who was so sensitive on the phones. Together, they saved many lives. They worked late into the night in the Seattle Crisis Clinic, which was housed in an old Victorian House on Capitol Hill.

When at age fourteen, two of my friends and I went to a 1972 Rolling Stones concert at the Seattle Coliseum, my mom did not want us to wait for the bus afterward. She picked us up and brought us back to the Crisis Clinic, where "we would be safe with her and Ted."

When we were introduced to Ted, my friends, Janell and Teresa, thought he was "cute." I was not impressed. I can't quite put my finger on what it was, but there was something about him that I secretly thought of as "icky."

Ted would not meet my eyes. He and my mother went to the other room where they sat and talked and waited for the phones to ring, and my friends and I played Chinese checkers as they gushed about Ted.

The old Victorian house has been torn down and the Crisis Clinic moved to another location. Today a facility for the mentally ill sits on the spot where Ann and Ted once answered the phones.

"If any place is haunted, it is probably that site," Ann said.

We do not know if Ted was killing during his stint at the Crisis Clinic. We know only that teenage girls around Seattle began to vanish in the mid-1970s. Ann got a contract to write her very first book about the disappearances. In another bizarre coincidence, she had no idea that her friend Ted Bundy would turn out to be the killer.

Ted took two girls from Lake Sammamish State Park on July 14, 1974. And while one girl never spoke with her loved ones again, the other may have done so *after* he took her life.

When Denise Naslund's mother, Eleanore Rose, and I collaborated on an article about Denise's death for *Woman's World* magazine in the summer of 1992, she was still haunted by that awful day eighteen years before. "Denise had been invited to Lake Sammamish," Eleanore told me. "She said there was going to be a picnic with games and prizes. I said, 'It sounds like fun,' but she said she didn't feel like going. I told her, 'Don't go if you don't want to.'"

If only she *hadn't*.

Lake Sammamish State Park saw forty thousand people crowding its beach that sunny Monday as sunbathers and picnickers spread out blanket to blanket.

A young man with his arm in a sling approached pretty girls and asked for help loading his sailboat onto his car. Witnesses did not report seeing Denise Naslund leave with him, but a few saw petite, blonde Janice Ott agree to help. They overheard him give his name as Ted.

The arm in the sling had been a predator's ruse and it was obvious that Denise had been fooled just as Janice had.

Eleanore looked so sad as she described her last morning with Denise. She shook her head, remembering her lovely, sweet dark-haired daughter, who had now been gone as many years as she had been alive. She said good-bye to her eighteen-year-old daughter for the last time on a hot July day.

When I visited in 1992, Denise's 1963 Chevrolet was still parked outside her mother's home, a silent memorial to the vivacious teenager. And Denise's room was untouched—her stuffed animals scattered on her bed, her clothes still hanging in the closet.

Was Denise's spirit there? Perhaps. There was a palpable sadness in that room. It may have been Denise, or it may have been the overwhelming cloud of her mother's grief. Eleanore, too, is gone now and I hope mother and daughter had a joyful reunion.

It was Janice, the kind-hearted young woman who always helped those in trouble, who reached out from the other side. Just 100 pounds and five feet tall, her family described the twenty-three-year-old as idealistic. It was only natural that she would assist someone who appeared disabled.

Her husband, Jim, was in California taking a course, and had no idea his wife did not come home from the lake that day. In fact, he would not hear that she was missing until Tuesday morning.

Yet Monday night, before he had an inkling that anything was wrong, he fell asleep as he waited by the phone for Janice to call.

He came abruptly awake at 10:45 P.M.

"I heard her voice," he later told Ann Rule. "I heard it as clearly as if she was in the room with me. She was saying, 'Jim . . . Jim . . . Come help me! . . .'"

Eleanore Rose in her daughter's bedroom in 1992. She left daughter Denise Naslund's room exactly as it was when she said good-bye to her for the last time on a summer morning in 1974. (Leslie Rule)

Denise and Janice were found together, so long after their spirits had vacated their bodies there was little evidence left for detectives. Perhaps the girls helped each other through the ordeal. I hope so.

After murdering many more young women and girls, Theodore Bundy was executed on January 24, 1989. There is no one left alive to tell the details of Denise's and Janice's last moments.

The last words were spoken from beyond by Janice.

They echo hauntingly. *Come help me!*

Peace be with you, Janice.

Ted's murderous rampage covered at least three states. The teenage girls were all lovely with long hair parted in the middle. Unbelievably, Ted escaped from jail twice in the middle of the sad saga, each time killing again.

When Ted Bundy was executed, he took many secrets to his grave. He did not confess to all the killings, nor did he tell where the bodies could be found.

Ghost stories swirl around the Bundy case—including undocumented ghost sightings of his youngest victim.

Poor little Anne Marie Burr is thought by many to have been Ted's first victim. In 1961, the child was just nine years old and she followed teenage Ted around like a puppy dog. He was her neighbor and the paperboy—someone she trusted.

Anne Marie was a sweet little girl who loved butterflies and music. She took piano lessons from Ted Bundy's uncle. She often got up early in the morning to practice the piano. She disappeared from her Tacoma, Washington, home on the morning of August 16, 1961. A window and the front door were found open.

Had she left on her own? Or had someone come in and taken her?

The agonizing questions are still unanswered for her family. Anne Marie was never found. She would likely have been a grandmother by now.

The street by her house was being worked on at the time of her disappearance, and it is possible that she was hidden beneath it. Many area people say they think she is hidden in the foundation of a building on the campus of the University of Puget Sound. It is here that rumors of ghost sightings abound. The story goes that the ghost of a little girl is seen walking the halls of the building and that inexplicable odd noises are heard.

Viewmont High School in Bountiful, Utah, is also rumored to be haunted by the horror of a Bundy abduction. On the night of November 8, 1974, seventeen-year-old Debby Kent was taken from the parking lot as her parents sat inside the school watching a student production of *The Redhead*. Witnesses heard two terrified screams and saw Ted's Volkswagen racing from the parking lot.

Thirty years have passed, and Debby has not been found.

True or not, stories circulate about sightings of a ghostly scenario in the parking lot. The Volkswagen, Ted, and Debby are said to be seen there. If so, it is probably not ghosts, but a place memory imprinted upon the environment. As mentioned before, this is the phenomenon of a dramatic event that is somehow held by the atmosphere, played back again and again so witnesses can actually view it as they would a movie.

A Face for a Ghost

Ghost enthusiasts agree. Murder victims *want* their cases solved. And while homicide investigators and forensic experts are often hesitant to mention the paranormal events that surround their work, some privately admit that they may have had just a little help from someone on "the other side" in solving a crime.

Little Aliyah Davis did not have a chance. Five and a half years old and living in West Philadelphia in 1981, her fate was in the hands of her mother, Maria Davis Fox. The court had given Maria custody of her children—despite the fact she was serving an eight-year probation for the 1974 beating death of her baby son.

Aliyah's big sister, eight-year-old Amira, was afraid of her mother and her stepfather, Charles Fox, who sometimes stabbed and starved the children. She wished she could protect Aliyah, her cute little sister, who wore two pigtails and smiled so sweetly. The family was watching *Dukes of Hazzard* on television, when Aliyah had an accident in her pants. Amira and her siblings watched helplessly as Charles beat their little sister to death.

Years went by, and no one seemed to notice or care that Aliyah was not with the family while Maria and Charles continued to collect welfare checks for the murdered girl.

It must have seemed to Amira that the killers would never be punished for what they had done to her sister. Then again, she had known and loved Aliyah for five and a half years. Perhaps she knew her sister had an invincible spirit—one that could not be stopped by death.

While world-famous forensic sculptor Frank Bender tends to be skeptical when it comes to ghost stories, he has no explanation for the unusual assistance he received in a heartbreaking case.

It is as if by magic that Frank's sensitive fingers coax features from the clay that covers the unidentified skulls. The finished heads are so lifelike that you can't help but jump when you first see them staring at you. Yet it is not the fact that Frank Bender is a talented artist that is so incredible. It is his uncanny ability to give something precious back to the dead. *Their faces.*

Classically trained at the Pennsylvania Academy of Fine Arts, Frank did not set out to become a "Recomposer of the Decomposed," the job

Frank Bender with his first reconstructed face. His accuracy resulted in a killer's conviction. (Leslie Rule)

title his answering machine gives. In the mid-1970s, while researching anatomy, he toured the Philadelphia medical examiner's office and viewed an unidentified woman who was killed when shot in the head and her features were lost. Moved by the victim's plight, Frank reconstructed her face, a procedure that requires sterilizing the skull and covering it with clay to sculpt a new face. Once finished, a mold is made from the original, and a copy is made.

Frank's first forensic sculpture resulted in the identification of Anna Mary Duval from Phoenix and her killer was convicted. Frank Bender has since created dozens of forensic sculptures with nearly as many cases solved as a result. In addition to recomposing victims, he does age projection—including one on the widely publicized fugitive John List, who hid for nearly two decades after murdering his family. When *America's Most Wanted* featured the bust of List, the likeness was so exact that the fugitive was captured eleven days later.

How does the sculptor take a skull and give it the semblance of the person it once belonged to, complete with the right hair, wrinkles, correctly colored eyes, and style of eyeglasses?

Good question. Frank has his share of scientific answers, and would rather use the word "intuition" than "psychic." Yet he can take a shattered skull with the features obliterated by a weapon and re-create the exact nose, lips, and eyes over a gaping hole.

Once a face has been recomposed, you can almost see the dignity restored in the eyes. Some of these faces are lined up on shelves in Frank's Philadelphia studio. There is a calm and challenging air about them. They seem to be daring their killers to try to get away with murder.

Each bust takes hundreds of hours to complete. It is a labor of love he does for the lost ones, the victims who are so callously thrown away. When he stops to do the math, he earns pennies per hour. His satisfaction comes from knowing that many a Jane or John Doe recover their names, and their killers are stopped from hurting others.

It is the children who bother him the most. In 1982, Philadelphia road workers made a sad discovery beneath the Platt Memorial Bridge. "They found a steamer chest with a body in it," said Frank, explaining that the men waited to call the police. They saw the human remains wrapped in a garbage bag and sheets, but pawed through the contents, hoping to find something worth money. "They completely destroyed the crime scene," he said.

She was a child of color, about five years old. But authorities had no clues to her identity. Frank went to work, his gentle fingers forming a tiny upturned nose. He worked for hours, but the right face simply would not emerge from the clay. He was unaccustomedly stumped and frustrated.

"That night I had a dream," he told me. "I was walking down a long corridor that led to a morgue," he said, describing the scene in detail right down to the shade of beige on the walls. The doors to the morgue were open, and there was nothing but darkness beyond. A gurney sat blocking the doorway, upon it a little girl. "She sat up and smiled at me," said Frank. "Her skin was so beautiful, dark with a reddish hue, and she wore two pigtails."

He studied the soft curve of her cheeks, the tilt of her nose, and her wide brown eyes. He woke up energized, the child's gaze burned into his memory, her smile urging him to get to work. "I knew it was her. I knew it was right," he said.

Frank Bender with the reconstruction of the face of a little girl. He helped convict her killers. (Leslie Rule)

Dream Visits

It is a widely held theory that spirits can insert themselves into dreams. Dreamers can distinguish between a dream event and an actual spirit visit by the intensity and vividness of the experience.

A spirit visit within a dream leaves a lasting impression on the dreamers, who may find themselves thinking, *It was so real!* This type of ghost encounter is especially common when it comes to lost loved ones, particularly within the time frame of a recent death. Most people find these experiences reassuring.

It is thought that the dreamers are in such a relaxed and open state while asleep that they are able to make a psi connection with a disembodied soul that they may resist during waking time.

Psychic people tend to have this type of spirit visit more often than others and will often connect with spirits of those they don't know. In some cases, the departed folks need to get a message across and choose a psychic as a conduit. Many of these types of spirit visits have been reported in the cases of unsolved deaths.

Though the dream had lasted only seconds, it had been so vivid that Frank remembered every detail. He completed the sculpture, duplicating the image of the dream girl, right down to the two cute pigtails that stuck out from the sides of her head.

A photograph of the bust was put on flyers and distributed to police stations. It was there that some six years later a visitor happened to glimpse one of the flyers. Ronald Davis was taken aback as he recognized his daughter, Aliyah, whom he had lost custody of when courts gave her to his murderous ex-wife.

The proverbial wheels of justice finally began to turn and soon Charles Fox and Maria Davis Fox were arrested. Fifteen-year-old Amira was the star witness for the state.

Maria was sentenced to ten to twenty years and Charles got fifteen to forty.

Ronald, Aliyah's biological father, was overcome by the uncanny likeness Frank had created of his little girl. "He wanted to know how I knew about the pigtails, and how I got her skin shade right," said Frank.

It seems he had help from a spunky little spirit.

How Sweet the Sound

Amazing Grace, how sweet the sound . . .

When Lynn Mueller sang "Amazing Grace" it was indeed a sweet sound.

"It was her favorite song," remembered one of her friends, artist Norma Jean Campanaro. Lynn sang it so beautifully that the memory still brings tears to Norma Jean's eyes.

Lynn has been gone for nearly three decades now. Few people speak of the vibrant young woman whose strong voice once filled the lovely old church on East Main Street in Ventura, California. Most folks in Ventura probably don't remember her name. They may recall that a shocking murder occurred on East Main Street, but they don't know the details. Oddly, news accounts of the brutal killing were brief.

The local newspaper reported there was "a strict news blackout ordered by Assistant District Attorney Michael Bradbury." The Muellers' friends and acquaintances and the police were forbidden to speak to reporters.

All these years later, the public is still in the dark about much of the case.

Born Lynn Marie Balducci on November 5, 1953, in St. Louis, Missouri, she had lived on East Main Street just two months, yet it is *there*, her spirit remains. As mentioned in the previous chapter, the haunted Victorian Rose B&B is housed in an old church. In 1975, Lynn was a happily married twenty-one-year-old who lived next door to the church and worshiped there with her husband. Their house was a small rental and their landlord applauded them as "excellent tenants" who were excited about painting and landscaping.

The Victorian Rose owner, Richard Bogatch, said that the ghost of Lynn frequently manifests there, sometimes in mirrors. "Guests report seeing Lynn in the loft. That's where the choir sang," he confided.

Before joining the church, the Muellers had lived a fun lifestyle as

Ghosts in the News

Through the Looking Glass

AN AMERICAN MEDIA WEEKLY NEWSPAPER reported that the prime suspect in a case that shocked our nation saw the ghost of his wife just days after she vanished in December 2002. As of this writing, Scott Peterson, a thirty-year-old Modesto, California, fertilizer salesman, is still on trial for the murder of his pregnant wife, Laci, twenty-seven, and their unborn son, Connor. The bodies of mother and baby washed ashore in the spring of 2003 in Richmond, California. The nation mourned as videos of Laci during happy times were broadcast. The vivacious brunette wore a perpetual grin, and the footage of her clowning around with her friends captured the hearts of Americans who grieved for the mother-to-be and the child who would never know life.

The news account cited a police report that said Scott told Laci's friend Kim McNeely about his startling encounter with the spirit of his missing wife.

While asleep in the home where prosecutors contend that he murdered Laci, Scott suddenly awoke in the middle of the night. He got out of bed and as he glanced into a mirror, he saw the ghost of Laci standing behind him.

(Source: American Media, Boca Raton, Florida)

entertainers. But the church frowned upon such things as rock and roll, television, and short skirts. "Lynn loved the Lord," stressed Norma Jean. "She joined the church because she thought it was right."

For the last two and a half years of her life, Lynn embraced her new religion.

Sometimes when guests at the Victorian Rose see the apparition in the matronly skirt with her hair pulled back in a bun, they assume it is the ghost of an older woman. But Norma Jean points out that Lynn, as dictated by the strict codes of her church, dressed in the frumpy fashion of an old lady.

Lynn was vivacious with much love to give, and by all rights, should have had many years ahead to give it. She taught Sunday school and the children flocked around her, mesmerized by the kind teacher who always had a hug for a little one. She would have been a wonderful mother.

On a May evening in 1975, while her husband was at work, Lynn was viciously attacked and stabbed. The murder was so ugly that ambulance drivers were not allowed near the scene.

"Her husband was devastated," remembered Norma Jean.

It was the worst murder in the history of Ventura and frightened citizens were anxious to know who was responsible. But weeks slipped by with no answers. The weeks turned to months and the months to years.

A killer has gotten away with murder.

And a persistent spirit clings to a place she loved. When Norma Jean heard that Lynn's ghost was still seen at the Victorian Rose she formed a prayer circle there, hoping to help the restless soul cross over.

But Lynn's ghost still appears at the B&B. It is as if she won't leave until justice is served. Norma Jean strengthened her resolve to find that justice for her friend. "I've been to the police station many times over the years," said Norma Jean. "They have nothing new to tell me."

Witnesses have shared information with this writer that the police were previously unaware of. (If the killer is reading this, he should be aware that these witnesses have relocated and would be difficult for him to find. Their signed testimony is in a safe deposit box.)

What is this compelling information?

A male authority figure in the church was known to "punish" female members for actions he deemed inappropriate. For obvious reasons, details here will be vague and I will call him Mr. Weeds.* Mr. Weeds "punishment" was so humiliating that even today these witnesses are traumatized when they speak of it.

Is it possible that Lynn was being "punished" by Mr. Weeds when she met her violent death?

Another disturbing fact has also risen. A little girl among the parishioners, who spent time with Mr. Weeds, attempted suicide. What would make a child so upset that she would choose death? Was she tangled up in a controversy that led to Lynn's murder?

Did Lynn intervene on the child's behalf? Is that why she was so swiftly silenced? Was that her punishment for speaking up for a child?

The night of Lynn's murder, a church member was giving a party and Lynn called to say she could not attend. Mr. Weeds, too, was conspicuously absent from the party. He was, however, present at the funeral.

The church was packed, and the pitiful wailing of the children who loved Lynn punctuated the sadness. So many cried, yet one among them could have been weeping crocodile tears.

The killer could have been a stranger. Mr. Weeds might be nothing more than a cruel man. But that is not for me to decide. It is the job of the homicide detectives and perhaps with the publication of this book, they will again pick up the investigation and look at these new leads. Maybe this murder will finally be solved.

. . . *Yea, when this flesh and heart shall fail,*
And mortal life shall cease,
I shall possess, within the veil,
A life of joy and peace.

As in the words of Lynn Mueller's favorite song, maybe *then* she can find peace.

---

* Whenever an asterisk appears, names have been changed to protect privacy.

The Lost Lady

I work in the PECO Energy building, in Coatesville and several times, when I'm in here very early (I know this sounds strange) a ghostly lady with wet hair and a gold spot on the top of her dress comes through. She's very forlorn . . .

So began the e-mail I received on February 7, 2002. It came from a stranger. She was not a reader of my books and she was not a reader of my mother's books. In fact, she had never heard of either of us.

Katie Furman was so troubled by her encounters with the sad ghost that she got on her computer and went to the Web for help. She entered two words into "Search."

"Crime" and "Ghosts."

With the miracle of the World Wide Web she was connected to my mother's Web site address where she found my e-mail address and seconds later sent me a note, describing the pitiful spirit.

She ended her e-mail asking, *Was someone killed here?*

It is amazing that two strangers can meet at their desks, hundreds of miles apart on opposite coasts of the country. Katie is a couple of hours from Philadelphia, Pennsylvania, and I live near Seattle, Washington. And yet what a *small* world. My mom went to high school in Coatesville.

Katie and I quickly formed an Internet friendship. She told me that she had seen the ghost three times and each time the scenario was the same:

It is summertime and Katie arrives before 4:00 A.M., long before dawn's cold light can creep over the building. She is always alone in her cubicle when a woman with wet hair comes down the hallway, stops in the doorway and peers in at her.

The first time Katie saw her, she thought that it was her fellow employee Mary Grace arriving at work. Concerned that something was wrong, Katie jumped up and ran after her down the hallway. "But she was gone," said Katie. "Mary Grace came in a while later."

An overwhelming sadness accompanies the encounters. "She seems forlorn, but she knows I am here," confided Katie. "I can tell. She stops in the doorway and looks at me. There is a gold patch of light on the middle of her dress over the breast. The dress seems blue-gray, as does the lady."

The spirit "moves smoothly and quietly. She goes down the aisle and then I can't see her anymore. Now that I know she's dead, I stay in my seat and don't run after her anymore."

Katie, a devout Catholic, said three rosaries for the spirit, and though she did not see her again, she could not stop thinking of her.

I urged her to talk to the old-timers who worked in the building, to ask if any of them knew of a nearby traumatic death of a young woman.

I soon received an e-mail back from Katie saying that a coworker told her that an unidentified body had been found a few years before not quite two miles from the building where she had seen the ghost. She got on a police Web site and read the details of the Jane Doe.

"I was horrified to see her legs were found very far away from her," said Katie, who explained that the ghost's legs, too, were missing. Though this is sometimes the case with apparitions, it was a chilling coincidence.

In another coincidence, a friend of my mom's, forensic sculptor Frank Bender, had done a reconstruction of the victim's face. To make a long story short, I soon flew to Philadelphia to investigate. Moved by the plight of the unidentified victim and the possible connection to the sad spirit that Katie saw, I knew this was something I had to write about.

The Embreeville Police Department graciously allowed us to stop by. "They want to solve the case and need the publicity to do that," said Frank, and tactfully added, "But I don't think you should mention ghost stories."

I understood. Not everyone believes in ghosts. And some people believe that those who *do* are unbalanced. So I followed Frank's advice and did not mention that the writing project I was working on involved the paranormal. I listened as Frank and Corporal Mark Healey did most of the talking. The skull was brought out of the evidence room and I watched Frank handle it as he recalled the sculpture he had made several years before when he had covered it with clay. A mold had been made from the original bust and a copy made before the skull was cleaned and returned to the evidence room.

Corporal Healey took us to the spot where the victim was found alongside the Brandywine Creek on Valley Creek Road. It is a lightly treed area beside a railroad trestle, a place where teenagers sometimes go to drink beer. Broken bottles littered the inside of the abandoned tunnel that looked out onto the site.

Frank Bender stands in the mouth of a tunnel at the scene where a victim was discarded in a suitcase in Pennsylvania. (Leslie Rule)

The woman had been found in a maroon suitcase, on July 11, 1995, and had died an estimated three to seven days before. Corporal Healey showed us the puddle of water where she had been, face down, zipped inside the suitcase.

Despite the horror that had been discovered there, the scene felt peaceful. A little frog bobbed to the surface of the puddle and peeked out at us, and wildflowers speckled the area.

Corporal Healey pointed up the hill to the train tracks. "She might have been thrown out of the train," he told us. He had spent long hours examining every probable angle. He'd also investigated the possibility that the victim was connected to a carnival that had been in town around the time of her death, or that she had been on her way to a nearby summer camp, perhaps seeking work as a camp counselor.

The woman had brown eyes and brown hair, appeared to be between twenty-five and thirty-five years old, and was probably between four eleven and five three, weighing between 120 and 140 pounds. She had a dead tooth, pierced ears, and no scars or tattoos. She had never given birth. Her legs were found miles away in January 1996.

Forensic sculptor Frank Bender and Corporal Mark Healey with the reconstruction of a Jane Doe. Is it her ghost who is seen crying in a nearby building? (Leslie Rule)

It is our hope that a reader will recognize the victim from Frank Bender's reconstruction, that "the Lost Lady" will find her name, so she can be put to rest. And *perhaps* a killer will be caught.

Did the spirit Katie encountered belong to the Brandywine Creek Jane Doe?

Katie said the reconstruction of the victim looked similar to the ghost she saw, though the ghost appeared to have lighter hair. (But then, the whole appearance of the apparition was the color of bleached denim. Spirits often appear as white or ice blue.) Katie also pointed out that the victim was found with a denim shirt with brass buttons and wonders if one of those buttons was the shiny light she saw on the ghost's chest.

If indeed the ghost and the victim are one and the same, then the spirit did not have to wander far to find someone who could see her. "The Lost Lady" chose Katie and Katie found me. As a result, the story of a woman who was thrown away is an open book for the world to read.

Now it is a reader's turn to pick up the thread of this sad story and help "the Lost Lady" find her way home.

For more information on this unidentified woman, others like her, and missing people, visit the Doe Network at www.doenetwork.org.